Botty's
RULES

Botty's RULES

29 success secrets from the
UK entrepreneur who's been
there and done it …

NIGEL BOTTERILL

Vermilion
LONDON

1 3 5 7 9 10 8 6 4 2

Published in 2011 by Vermilion, an imprint of Ebury Publishing
A Random House Group Company

First published in the US in 2011 by Glazer-Kennedy Publishing
An imprint of Morgan James Publishing

The Random House Group Limited supports the Forest Stewardship Council® (FSC®),
the leading international forest certification organisation. All our titles that are printed on
Greenpeace approved FSC® certified paper carry the FSC® logo. Our paper procurement
policy can be found at www.randomhouse.co.uk/environment

MIX
Paper from
responsible sources
FSC® C016897

Designed and set by seagulls.net

Printed in the UK by CPI Mackays, Chatham, ME5 8TD

ISBN 9780091939922

To buy books by your favourite authors and register for offers visit
www.randomhouse.co.uk

This is a work of non-fiction. In some cases the names and identifying characteristics of
individuals have been changed to protect their privacy.

For Sue, without whom this story really wouldn't have happened. She's amazing. xx

CONTENTS

INTRODUCTION

This book tells a story ... and also serves as a reference tool for those running their own businesses.

The story is about a guy from Leeds who, in 2002 at the age of 36, stepped off the corporate ladder to do his own thing. Married, with children and a big mortgage, he set up his own business.

Less than four years later he was a millionaire.

In the last five years he has built five separate million-pound-plus businesses from scratch.

This book is the story of how he did it; of what worked well and what went wrong; his successes and triumphs; his mistakes and cock-ups.

Interwoven throughout the story are **Botty's Rules**: the key lessons that he has learnt on his journey and collectively they are a blueprint for super-success in twenty-first-century business and a crucial reference tool for any business owner who wants to make it big.

This is my story.

These are my rules.

I hope, sincerely, that you both enjoy ... and prosper.

CHAPTER 1
HOW IT ALL STARTED ...

1966 was a great year for English football. I was six months old, sitting on my father's knee when, right at the end of extra time of the World Cup Final against West Germany, Geoff Hurst scored the fourth goal to seal the trophy for England. My dad jumped up, threw me in the air and my head hit the ceiling.

Let's just say, it took my mum a long time to forgive him.

Some say that bang on my head has a lot to do with what's happened since ...

I grew up in a very happy home in Halton, a suburb to the east of Leeds. My dad John had been a police constable for many years and just after I was born, he found his ambition, and started getting promoted quite regularly. He made it to Assistant Chief Constable in West Yorkshire Police before retiring in 1991 at the age of 55.

Having a dad who was a policeman was quite a cool thing as a kid. In my early teens especially, it made me very popular. He used to come home from work in the big traffic car with all the lights and sirens and park it in the drive. My friends would come around and we'd crawl all over his police car.

Dad was quite an inspiration to me. He'd grown up in East Yorkshire in a very small farming community where no one ever had ever left to go to the 'big city'. He was the first in his family to ever get out of Nafferton, the little village where they lived. It was a big thing.

He came to the bright lights of Leeds, joined the police and went on to have a very successful career.

My mum Pamela worked as a telephonist before she had me and my younger sister. As was traditional back then, she was a stay-at-home mum. When I was nine she became a dinner lady at my school, which was just about the worst thing she could ever have done to me. You see, while having a dad who brought police cars home was very cool, it was very uncool for your mother to be the school dinner lady.

An Eight-Day Coma

I can't tell this story without telling you that it almost never happened. On Christmas Day, 1974, I caught German measles. A few days later, my dad was working an early shift. It was around 5 a.m. when he was getting ready for work and something made him put his head round my bedroom door. He found something pretty horrific. I was unconscious. I had had some type of seizure; I'd swallowed my tongue and even with his first-aid training, he couldn't revive me.

The ambulance came and I was rushed to hospital. It was touch and go. At one point it looked like I'd died.

I eventually came round over a week later, on my ninth birthday on 9 January 1975. I'd been in a coma for eight days. I'd contracted a rare virus called encephalitis, which is an inflammation of the brain.

Of course, it was much more traumatic for my parents and sister than it was for me. My sister Elizabeth (if I want to really annoy her, I call her Betty) is younger than me, so to see your big brother being carried away by ambulance, with no one knowing whether I was going to make it, was pretty hard for her. I was out of school for many months, then back on only half days for quite a while. I was the first patient in Yorkshire to come through encephalitis completely unscathed.

There was another child at the same time, in the hospital with the same disease. He had major disabilities for the rest of his life. I was lucky. All I was left with, bizarrely, was asthma!

First Job and my Inspirational Uncle Gordon

Growing up in Leeds in the '60s and '70s, was okay. We weren't wealthy, by any means, but neither were we poor – and my football team was the best in the world! And I remain a loyal and devoted fan of Leeds United to this day. Life was good. We lived in a modern three-bedroom semi and I had a happy childhood, much of which revolved around the Methodist church and the Boys' Brigade. At school, I acquired the nickname 'Botty'. Not the most flattering or creative nickname ever, but I didn't mind, and it stuck.

In my teens, my uncle Gordon, who was an accountant in Driffield, was a major influence on my life. He had a big house, he drove big flashy cars and when Leeds United were playing in Europe, he got tickets to all the matches.

He was an inspirational figure to me. I just remember thinking that I'd rather have a life like my uncle Gordon than like Mum and Dad's, so there was a drive within me to have material success. It came from him.

I'm very proud of my Yorkshire roots. My love of cricket and Leeds United were bred in me from a very early age, as was my strong work ethic.

I'd only just turned 13 when I came home from school one day and my mum told me that she'd got me a job. I wasn't aware that she was looking for a job for me or, indeed, that I needed one. But she told me that Mr Schofield, who ran the local paper shop, had a vacancy for a paper round, and she'd secured it for me.

I earned the princely sum of £1.20 a week. I delivered 89 copies of the *Yorkshire Evening Post* to homes in our neighbourhood. It was my first experience of work.

I actually quite enjoyed it and after a few weeks I took on a morning paper round as well. I've always been a morning person – even today I do my best work as dawn is breaking – and I really enjoyed getting up at 6 a.m. My little transistor radio was usually with me. Of course, I couldn't play it too loud because it woke up people, but I kept it quite close to my ear so I could enjoy some music and the news bulletins as I delivered the papers.

Some memorable things happened during those early morning paper rounds with my radio. One day, I heard them say that one of the Beatles had died, but I had to wait half an hour until the next news bulletin to find out which one it was. Of course it turned out to be John Lennon who had been shot and killed in New York.

Another memorable day was when they caught the Yorkshire Ripper, which was a big deal in Leeds at that time. For much of my childhood, the spectre of the serial killer we now know was Peter Sutcliffe loomed large over West Yorkshire.

A Safe and Secure Job

During this time, I was quite diligent at Temple Moor, an all-boys' comprehensive. I found school quite straightforward and there was nothing really remarkable that happened to me. I was able to get nine O levels when I was 16 years of age and everyone expected that I would go back to school, study my A levels and then go on to university. But I had other ideas.

My work ethic was very strong, remember. Neither of my parents had been to university. I was the first in my family to get a bunch of O levels, but I was quite keen to get out there into the workplace rather than go back to school and university, and my parents actively encouraged this.

It was 1982, so we were in the depths of the Thatcher recession and unemployment was soaring. Looking back, for a 16-year-old I had quite a sad outlook on life. I'm not really sure how much this was me and how much of it was my parents, to be honest, but I decided it would be a good idea to leave school and get a job with a bank.

What everyone tells you when you're that age is that you work hard at school, pass your exams and then you get a job. I thought, 'Well, I've worked hard at school and I've passed my exams, so I'd better get a job. That's what you do.' If only I'd known then what I know now, things might have been very different ...

I decided that banking looked like the right thing for me (I was very, very unself-aware at that age) so I applied to a whole bunch of banks in Leeds. Barclays wrote back and asked me for an interview.

I went to the interview wearing my school uniform because I didn't have a suit. The gentleman that interviewed me was David Styles. I remember him asking me what the reason was that I wanted to work in a bank. Please remember that I was just 16 years old at this point. To my eternal embarrassment, I told him that I wanted to work in a bank because 'It was a very safe and secure job.' (I'm cringing as I write this, believe me, but it's true!)

It's very sad that as a 16-year-old I was thinking about security of tenure over anything else in life – which I think gives insight into the very conservative kind of environment that'd I'd grown up in. Work hard, pass your exams, get a job, work 40 years and retire with a pension.

The interview process took a few weeks and I'd just gone back to school to start my A level course when Barclays offered me a job. So it was with great delight I went into school and announced to my teachers that I was going to leave. It was genuinely quite a shock to them.

All except one of my friends were staying on to do A levels, so for me to leave was really quite a rebellious thing at that point in my life. It was just expected by my teachers and friends that I would stay on for an extra couple of years. I had conversations with people saying, 'Well, at least I've got a job now.' I was just so terribly insecure at that age and felt this was my opportunity to get a job and that I needed to be happy and take it.

I walked away from school at the beginning of October 1982, and I started work at Barclays. It was the week that Channel 4 began broadcasting in the UK and my first day at work was the day after they raised the *Mary Rose*, Henry VIII's flagship. I remember my mum taking me down to the local Marks & Spencer, where she bought me a couple of suits. One was a nice, brown-checked suit, very de rigueur, and the other a grey pinstriped one, which looked, frankly, ridiculous on a 16-year-old boy with acne, but it was what it was.

I began work as an office junior at Barclays Bank on Albion Street in Leeds. My first payslip was £116.16, which at the time felt like a complete fortune. I had no idea how I could ever spend all that money. It was such a large amount. This was so much better than a paper round!

I stayed with Barclays for the next 18 years. I took to work quite well. My work ethic had prepared me. However, my first two years were by far the most formative of my life. While I was making the transition from school to work, all of my mates had gone back to school to study for their A levels; then they started dying. It was an unbelievable time. Andrew Tomlinson fell off of a mountain in the Lake District; Russell Lemon contracted leukaemia; as he came out of a pub after celebrating his mum's new marriage, Sean Dolan was knocked down and killed by a car that mounted the pavement. One kid threw himself under a train, two were killed in separate motorcycle accidents and six perished in a single car that rolled over and caught fire. I used to meet my friends at funerals.

It was a surreal time and, allied to my own experience with encephalitis a few years earlier, it meant that I came to terms with my own mortality at a very young age. Life is genuinely short.

'Just Give Me the Chequebook ...'

When I started at Barclays, I was the most junior person there, so I would do what anybody asked me to do. I was incredibly compliant and helpful, but I was also appallingly bad at paying attention to detail. I had one or two real nightmares in my early days at the bank.

One of the things I used to have to do was check all the account numbers on the internal vouchers when money was moved around. We had some big solicitor firms in Leeds banking at my branch at the time, and they used to move money around. I used to have to check that their numbers were all right, and I just got a little bit complacent.

I remember one day getting a call, and I had to walk across town to pick up this voucher because a big money transfer had gone wrong. I went to the solicitor's office to pick up the voucher and noticed when I picked it up that it was my mistake that had caused this. It was £100,000 that had been transferred into the wrong account, and it was my fault.

I remember walking back across Leeds on that Wednesday afternoon completely convinced that I was going to get sacked from my first real job. I wasn't fired, but they did extend my probation because of my lack of attention to detail. It was a big challenge and a wake-up call. I had a lot of sleepless nights in those early days at Barclays.

There were a few other incidents I won't forget, either. One day, I was walking out for lunch. I had just cut the wages for this customer, and as he walked down the steps of the bank ahead of me a youth pushed him over, hit him hard on the back of the head, grabbed his wages bag and ran off with it.

I was completely incensed by this, so I chased after the youth. I was quickly joined by three or four other people, and we chased this guy across Leeds city centre. He turned down a very narrow street and, amazingly, coming towards us in the opposite direction were two big, beefy police officers. We chased the culprit right into the arms of the law. He was arrested and justice was served.

I was elated and fulfilled by that, which was in direct contrast to an incident a couple of years later when I'd moved on to Leeds University branch. I came back from lunch one day and just got back to the counter when one of my colleagues, a lady named Janet (who loved to smoke very large cigars while in the office!) came and said, 'Nige, that's not Mr Brown,' pointing at this gent at the counter.

At that point, he knew he was caught and ran out of the branch. Janet explained that he was trying to cash a fraudulent cheque. I ran after him, but this time no one followed me. I was quite speedy in those days, and I quickly caught up with this guy in the middle of a shopping centre.

Approaching from behind, I put my hand on his shoulder and swung him round. As I did so, he pulled a knife, and we had a sort of stand-off. Here we were in the middle of a busy street with people all around. I remember it happening in almost slow motion.

I said the most ridiculous thing. I told him to just give me the chequebook. Amazingly, the guy did. He threw it down and ran off. I picked up the chequebook and walked back to the branch.

I was summoned to the regional office to account for my behaviour. The manager at the bank was very unhappy that I'd done this. I hadn't really thought about what I'd done at all; it was just out of instinct. He said to me, 'Nigel, you can't go chasing after customers like that.' I did point out to him that there was no evidence to suggest that he was actually a customer. I wasn't disciplined, but apparently it was a close-run thing. However, this incident brought me to the attention of some of the more senior people in Barclays in my local region.

There's definitely a lesson to be learnt here: there really is no such thing as bad publicity. A few weeks later I was invited to apply for a job in the regional office and I truly believe that if I hadn't run after the man with the fraudulent cheques, I'd never had been given the chance.

Sent to Coventry

At this point, I'd been with Barclays a few years, and I was very ambitious. I had one or two line managers who helped, nurtured and mentored me in those early days.

One in particular was a chap named Steven Fake. Steven was very instrumental in helping me realise that I actually had the ability and potential to have a successful career. He would put me forward for all sorts of opportunities and things that came along, including, on one occasion, sending me on an amazing three-week Outward Bound course in the Lake District. Unfortunately, I ended up being carried off the mountain and spent six days in Whitehaven Hospital, two of which were in intensive care. It was my worst experience ever with asthma and, apparently, at one point, I was in serious trouble.

Eventually, after serving my time at the regional office, I was put forward as a candidate to join Barclays' fast-track Management Development programme, which was a fast-track programme ostensibly for graduates. I was sent down to London as the Leeds region 'staff nominee' for that year and was successful.

This opened up all sorts of opportunities, but it meant that I had to move away from Leeds, because as part of this programme, you had to get experience in different parts of the company. So in 1990, when I was 24 years old, I moved south to the Midlands to work in Barclays' marketing department.

I'd done my research. Barclays had recently relocated their marketing department from London to Coventry. I'd already decided that there was no way I wanted to work in London. This was partly due to my conservative, parochial upbringing, partly due to the fact that I didn't want to move too far away from my family. So I took an interest in marketing, because marketing was based outside of London.

A couple of life-changing things happened in my first few weeks in Coventry. I started to learn the mechanics of marketing for the first time, and I met Sue Hall, the girl who would later become my wife.

I joined the project team that built and launched Barclays' first telephone banking business, Barclay Call, in 1992–93. At that time it was real cutting-edge stuff. We built one of the very first call centres ever in the UK.

When the project finished in November 1993, Sue and I went to Thailand on holiday but while we were there, I contracted appendicitis and ended up having my appendix removed under local anaesthetic in a shack by the beach. Sue thought I might die; I can confirm that it's weird having a conversation with a doctor while he removes one of your internal organs. However, 'all's well that ends well', as my grandma used to say. (My convalescence was set back markedly, though, when I called home and spoke to Dad, who told me that Leeds United had sold David Batty to Blackburn Rovers. That really upset me.)

Sue and I got married in April 1994 and shortly before the wedding, I landed another job within Barclays as an area sales manager in their Premier Banking division, responsible for the sales performance of 12 Premier Banking centres. Then something really important happened. I was invited for an interview to become the personal assistant to the Chief Executive of the UK Bank, a gentleman by the name of Richard Reay-Smith.

Richard and I hit it off immediately. With this job, I was left with no choice but to make the move to London. This was an amazing position where I had no direct responsibilities and no direct reports, but I had the ability to make anything happen within Barclays across the country. My roots were very much in the branches and at the grass-roots level at Barclays, but now I was privy to what was going on at the most senior level in the organisation.

Richard also sat me on the executive committee, and I was able to observe closely how a FTSE 100 company was run from the inside. To say it was a huge education for me just doesn't do it justice. It was a brilliant, brilliant place to be, and I learnt so much in the two years I worked in that role.

What was clear to me, sitting around the boardroom table with all the great and the good of the organisation, some hugely skilled, likable and very capable senior executives, was that the vision that they had for the bank and what they were trying to achieve all sounded fantastic. But, it was a visionary picture in a direction that was unknown to the staff working in the branches.

So I told 'em. I explained that there was a massive disconnect between what was going on in that boardroom and what was happening out there on the streets. They went into a little huddle and came back and told me that if this was a problem, then I'd better fix it.

Management Roles at Barclays

Every position I had at Barclays after I came out of the Management Development programme was a brand-new job that had never existed before and this was no exception. My new title was Communications Director. All of a sudden, I had responsibility for communication across the whole of Barclays in the UK. At one level, this was quite ridiculous because I was completely inexperienced. I was 29 years old and all of a sudden, I had this whole new level of massive responsibility.

This was an extremely fun time. Anyone working in Barclays around the mid-'90s will remember a series of events called 'The Power of One'. These were themed events where we'd pull together the managers from all across the country. It had never been done before.

We brought together hundreds of branch managers, where we gave them a whole lot of material and information to take back and share with their staff so we'd get the company messages down to the grass-roots level. That was the plan, anyway. The problem came when they didn't go back and share it with their staff; they kept it to themselves. Undeterred, we went down another level.

We moved to the Team Leader level. There was one particular week when we put on a series of events in three different venues across the country. We had three huge, 60,000-square-foot temporary structures that I had had built. There was one in the north-west at Haydock Park outside of Manchester, another in the Midlands at Stoneleigh near Coventry and the third down in the south-east at Brands Hatch, just outside the M25.

We ran the same events five days running and we brought 600 people a day into each of them. We put almost 10,000 members of the staff from Barclays through this whole event in the space of a week. It really was cutting-edge, radical stuff, and we rewrote the rulebook as we went along. It cost a fortune, but it had a massive impact on the culture of Barclays.

Looking back, without a doubt, it is the thing that I am most proud of from my time at Barclays. It had a big impact on the entire company, and all this was hugely formative for me. I started to realise that you can do new things, you can be different and you don't need permission for everything. I was loving it.

About this time Barclays started bringing external people into the organisation at the senior level. Until that point, they, like all the banks of the time, were a very old-fashioned and traditional organisation: the only people who got to senior jobs were those that had worked their way up from the bottom.

One such gentleman who was parachuted in at a top level was Malcolm Hewitt. Malcolm had the biggest influence on my career of anyone in Barclays. He was brought in to head up all the UK branches, particularly the revenue generation within those branches. He was a complete breath of fresh air in the company. He wasn't a banker. I forget now what his background was, but boy oh boy did he know his stuff when it came to motivating people and selling.

There were a few who were very resistant to any kind of change, but anyone with half a brain could see that the organisation needed to adapt and change. Most responded hugely well to Malcolm's leadership.

I got to know Malcolm very well and worked with him quite closely over my last couple of years at Barclays. He encouraged me to think bigger and to realise that I could do much more than I'd previously allowed myself to think I was capable of. He helped me discover a level of self-belief and confidence that I'd hitherto been unaware of, and he gave me the opportunity to tackle big jobs.

It was a big lesson for me. The importance of having someone who has been there and done it, guiding you, mentoring you, advising you, can be so powerful. Malcolm certainly fulfilled that role for me.

During that time at Barclays, we had an HR directive that executives at a certain senior level had to have a coach to help them develop. A lady, Frances White, who didn't work for Barclays, was brought in externally to coach some of the senior management team, including me.

I found myself having these one-on-one meetings with her and we got along very well. What happened over the course of four or five months, through my conversations with her and my relationship with Malcolm, was the realisation that I didn't really want to be at Barclays anymore. I'd been there 18 years at this point. There was just no way I wanted to stay and become a 'lifer' in the organisation.

I'd had a great run doing all these amazing things such as building call centres, driving cultural change, holding really big events and even building their first Internet banking service. It was an amazing career, but I was 34, and I *needed* to leave.

So at the end of 2000, after over 18 years with Barclays, I made the move and left all that I had known to that point.

Mobile Phones, Misery and the M6

I took a position working for a gentleman named John Caudwell. He's a bit more famous now than he was then, but he had built a formidable reputation.

He had built a huge mobile phone business from nothing. When I joined his team, the business was about 10 years old and was based in Staffordshire. John recruited me to be his Marketing Director at SinglePoint, which was his mobile phone airtime company.

This was a 'real' business. John offered me a lot of money. My starting salary was £120,000, and was my first six-figure salary, which, back in 2000, was a lot of money.

On the first day, I was to go and report to John's mansion in Staffordshire. We met in his kitchen to talk about the job and what we were going to do with it. It was winter, so it was quite a dark morning and dawn was breaking as I pulled into his driveway at around 7.30 a.m. He greeted me and then we walked to the kitchen. It was all very normal. He put on the kettle to make us some tea.

In many ways, working for John was the most miserable time of my career, but it was also one of the most educational periods because I learned a huge amount from him in the short time that I worked with him.

He'd built his business right across the supply chain in mobile phones, where the margins were extremely tight. He was making a small percentage, but he was making that percentage at every step through the supply chain and therefore building a very successful business.

As Marketing Director, I had something like 800 staff working for me. Part of my responsibility was the call centre. There was no training for any staff in the call centre. None whatsoever. So staff turnover was a big issue. On average, we had to recruit the entire workforce every year. Hardly anyone was staying longer than 12 months and many were leaving much sooner. It was a big problem that I had to address. What became very clear to me from my background at Barclays was that if we could give the staff the training they needed, they would perform better, which, in turn, would make them stay longer.

So a key plank of my plan to improve performance in my division was to get some training in place. We didn't have the capacity to keep a never-ending supply of the right people, but John just didn't see it that way.

He micro-managed everything that went on in that business. I remember once trying to order some pens. Here I was earning a six-figure salary, but I couldn't even order a £3.50 packet of 10 biros without it having to be signed off by John. I'd been brought in to do a job, but found it very difficult to do what I had been hired to do.

Looking back, I understand it more now that I've got my own business. John had a very small inner circle and between him and them, they controlled everything in that business. You can't fault them for that, because what they built was really quite extraordinary. In 2007, it was sold for over a billion pounds.

John did have a very different set of values to me, though, and that made it difficult for me to work with him. I didn't like the way he referred to his staff in private and our disagreement on whether staff should be trained or not was certainly a biggie.

Thing is, I was very much in isolation among his management team.

I still have a huge respect for John and all that he has achieved. He doesn't pretend to be anything that he isn't. He's true to his values, but in being true to mine, I just found it was an impossible working environment.

While working for John, I was commuting about 70 miles each way to work around the M6 – before the toll road was built. It was a 90-minute drive each way. Looking back, it's funny how you convince yourself that these things don't matter. I was completely seduced by the role, the salary and everything else. You convince yourself that it will be okay. This was a big lesson for me on how you can convince yourself of things that you know deep down are not right.

Eventually, after only a few months with John, I left. It was a very interesting departure. There was a board meeting where I was talking about my training plans. John looked at me across the table and said, 'Why should I spend my money on those people?'

I was completely and utterly exasperated. The silence was deafening. I remember standing up and realising that I had to leave. It was one of the most rebellious and liberating things I'd ever done in my life.

I walked slowly to the door and as I got there, one of the other directors at the table said, 'Oh, if you're leaving, can I have your car?' I'd been quite lucky when I arrived at the company, and the car I'd been allocated was a very swanky 7 Series BMW.

I peeled the key off my key ring and placed it on the corner of the table and went back to my office, where my secretary was waiting for me. I explained to her that I was leaving and asked if she could take me to the train station. I remember her saying, 'Oh, no, not again.' I was the fifth boss she'd had in the last 18 months.

I remember standing on the platform at Stoke Railway Station waiting to take the train ride home. This was a major setback for me because, up to that point, my career had gone amazingly well. I was 35 years of age, and I'd had no real major setbacks. I had been the golden boy at Barclays and now, within months of leaving, I was out of work. I remember thinking, 'It's how you respond to this that will be the making of you.'

Sue was there to support me, giving me a big hug when I got home. She didn't say anything, really, because she knew how unhappy I'd been. But the very next day, I figured I'd better find another job because at that point our new daughter, Tabitha, was only a few weeks old. I had a wife, three children, a big mortgage and an expensive lifestyle – but no job.

Back to Yorkshire … Three Days a Week

Amazingly, the very next day I found an ad on the Internet for a job with a company called CPP (Card Protection Plan) – and applications were closing that same day. Looking back, if I hadn't left Caudwell when I did I would never have seen this advertisement, and I would never have got the job that I did with CPP. The business was based in York, which was quite a hike.

What a great job it was at CPP. Once again I was working for a self-made entrepreneur: Hamish Ogston. In many ways, he is as equally successful as John Caudwell, but has a completely different style. Hamish built the CPP business over a number of years and he brought me in as the Managing Director to one of the three divisions.

He was a complete joy to work with, because he just let me get on with it and I was able to do what I wanted to do in my own way. This was a very liberating time in my career, because I was able to put into practice all the stuff that I'd learnt at Barclays and even what I'd learnt from Caudwell.

I stayed in York three days a week. I used to stay in a little hotel there called Mount Royale Hotel, so I was able to work 14–15-hour days, go back to the hotel and sleep. I used to go up on a Monday and drive back home on Thursday evening.

We delivered huge growth over the first couple of years. I mean, we *really* transformed that business and I took my division from a turnover of £3 million a year to £25 million in just a couple of years.

But working in York put a big strain on my family. I had three young children and I was away from home three nights a week. This really conflicted with my family values. It wasn't fun leaving the family for all that time, so, having done the job for two years, I decided I'd take the plunge and do something on my own.

I had a meeting in London with Hamish and Alan Blank, who was Hamish's right-hand man in the organisation. It was December 2002, and I told them that my plan was to leave the business the following year. I felt that the right thing to do was to give them six to nine months' notice, because they'd been very good to me. I'd enjoyed my time there, and we'd had a good relationship.

So at this review meeting with Hamish, I shared my plans with them. What happened then was really interesting and, once again, educational for me, because I was told that if that was my plan, I'd need to leave quite soon because the minute word got out (and it would) that I'd be going, I would become impotent as a Managing Director. When I started to think about it, I understood exactly where they were coming from.

So what was agreed upon at that meeting was very different from what I thought was going to be agreed upon. I thought I was being very good in letting them know I was going to leave in six months' time, but when I left the meeting, I found that I was leaving in four weeks, albeit with a very reasonable payoff. It was all very amicable. Hamish was very supportive to me.

I walked onto the concourse at Euston Station that day to catch the train home just thinking, 'Oh my God.' It's one thing to think about taking the plunge, but it's quite another to do it.

Rich Dad, Poor Dad

I went into WHSmith at Euston Station, and saw a book on the shelf called *Rich Dad, Poor Dad*. I thought, mistakenly as it turns out, that this morning I was a rich dad because I was on a very big salary with CPP and now I had no salary, so I was now going to be a poor dad. Of course, anyone who has read Robert Kiyosaki's book will understand that that's not the case at all.

I bought that book and read it on the train on the way back up to the Midlands. It confirmed my decision that I was now going to have to make it on my own.

Everyone that I knew tried to talk me out of it (*work hard, pass your exams, get a job*). No one in my family had ever run their own business.

None of my friends, at that point, had run their own business. All the people that I knew well were part of that established track where you go to school, get good exam results and then get a job.

Allied to this, I was also very aware that Sue and I had a very expensive lifestyle. Like most people, we'd got used to spending what we earned, and I had been very well paid.

So I needed to earn quite a lot of money. We couldn't survive on £20,000 or £30,000 a year. If I was going to have my own business, it would have to get quite big, quite quickly.

Throughout all of this, Sue was the lone person who stuck with me. She understood me. We had a great number of chats in the days following that meeting in London. The one question that I remember her asking me was, 'If you don't do this now, what will it feel like when you're 65?'

Answering that question made my decision easier. I haven't got many regrets in life but the few things I do regret are the things that I didn't do. I wasn't going to get another job; I was going to set out on my own.

The very next day I set up a company. It was really hard to find a name for it. I wanted a cool, trendy name and all the cool, trendy names I could think of were gone.

I went to see my accountant that day and in his office, there was a *Financial Times* in the reception. The front-page story that day was about a big conglomerate in the UK called R3, and I thought, 'That's a good name. If they can be called R3, I'll call my company N5.'

People say 'Oh, is the "N" for Nigel and "5" because there were five of you in the family?' Well it can, if you want it to be, but it actually wasn't. Honestly. It was just a letter and a number that came into my mind in my accountant's waiting room. I wish there was a better story, but there isn't. Sorry.

I set the company up, and N5 Ltd was formed. We started trading on 1 January 2003.

CHAPTER 2
I'M A CONSULTANT

At the risk of stating the bleedin' obvious – running your own home-based business is totally different to working for someone else.

It was a real shocker for me because my entire career had been spent in large organisations. I'd never even worked in a small company. All of a sudden, I was my own boss.

I decided I was going to be a consultant, mainly because I didn't know how to do anything else.

Sue and I made it work. I had a decent payoff from CPP, and we remortgaged our house, which freed up a chunk of money, and a modest pot of cash that I calculated gave me six or possibly seven months to make it work.

This meant that I had to get the business functioning quickly and it would have to be generating a five-figure monthly income – to replace my previous employed salary – within six months. That kind of goal really focuses your mind.

Something I found subsequently, as I've got to know a lot of entrepreneurs and business owners, is that it's the ones who *have* to make it work that tend to succeed the fastest and that certainly was my experience: I had to do it. Failure, quite simply, was not an option. I'd put everything on the line.

It was a big leap. I'd chosen to walk away from a corporate career, so whatever happened next was down to me. I figured I'd better get started.

First up, I had to buy a computer. I remember waiting until Boxing Day to take advantage of the sales so I could get the best value on the kit that I needed to set up my office. Straight after Christmas 2002, I jumped in with both feet. I was like a whirling dervish. I was busy, but boy did I waste time and energy. Looking back, I spent a lot of time in those early weeks doing what was, in hindsight, completely unimportant stuff.

For instance, I obsessed about creating a brochure for my new business, which was, frankly, an absurd thing to do given that I had no customers.

Bonkers Brochure and Bookkeeping

The most important thing for any new business is to get customers. And you get customers by getting out there selling – meeting people, talking about your business and how it can help them. You don't get any customers by creating brochures. I wish I'd known this in January 2003. I spent hours that month crafting and writing my brochure and getting a designer to lay it out beautifully. I spent over a grand getting hundreds of copies printed. It was a total waste of money.

The brochure never did anything for my business. It never got me a single lead or customer because brochures don't work. No one reads 'em.

I should have been out there selling, not fiddling about in my upstairs office, kidding myself I was being busy but in truth doing nothing at all to get my business moving. All that mattered was that I got customers, but I found distraction after distraction to divert my activities away from what mattered most into other, much less valuable stuff. I spent lots of time on unimportant things.

Another example was my bookkeeping. I invested hours of my time and lots of energy learning how to do my bookkeeping. Waste of time. I know now that you can get a really skilled bookkeeper for less than £20 per hour – and in my quest to generate a five-figure monthly income I could generate a lot more than £20 per hour if I got out there selling, but I didn't, not in those early days. It was over a year before I outsourced my bookkeeping. Should have done it on day one. Big mistake.

Having decided to offer my consultancy services to local businesses, I had to go out and get some clients, but I was very ill-equipped to do that. However, I was determined to make this work. I think one of my biggest strengths in those early months and years, and even today, is that I am eager and keen to learn. I was like a sponge in those early days, reading, studying and learning about other people that had made this journey before me – people who had built big successful businesses. I wanted to know what they'd actually done, because I figured that without any obvious talent, I was going to have to work really hard, and I needed all the help I could get.

I kept my attitude right. I'd tell myself every day in the mirror that I was a success. I talked a big game and got on with it, but it was difficult, especially working from home.

We had a three-storey house, so I set an office up on the top floor. I would go up there first thing in the morning and stay there until dinner time in the evening. The thing about working at home is that there are lots of distractions. You might think it's great to work at home, but it wasn't for me because I was never away from work and similarly you're never away from distractions when you're working, either.

A neighbour of mine used to work shifts. It wasn't long after I started up the business that I had a knock on the door

Botty's Rule No. 1
Take 100% responsibility.

As a business owner, you are 100% responsible for what happens to your business. It's all your fault ...
I've been accused of being too harsh with this rule. People say, 'Oh Nige, that's not true because X happened to my business.' I say, 'Rubbish.' It's all your fault.

Take the excellent BBC2 TV series *Mary Portas, Queen of Shops* as an example. Each week, retail guru Mary Portas turns up at some local shop that is on the verge of bankruptcy and completely transforms these businesses from struggling loss-making enterprises with few customers, into vibrant, popular, profit-making businesses. It's full of excellent lessons, not least of which is that *it is the business owner who is responsible for what happens to that business*. The greengrocer in Hoylake, for instance, blamed the arrival of the Sainsbury's Express shop for their performance, but Mary turned it round. Responsibility is a powerful thing. Think differently. Get out of your rut. Take responsibility.

I have a friend who runs a swimming pool business. The demand for swimming pools has shrunk massively during the recession and his business was about to go under. He saved himself by putting in place a maintenance programme to look after lots of the pools that he'd already installed. He is hanging in there because he took responsibility and created a new revenue stream. His two main competitors closed down, blaming the recession and everybody else but themselves. They avoided responsibility. It's not harsh. It's true.

one morning. It was my neighbour. He said he'd seen my car on the drive and had just come round for a coffee. This was a complete anomaly to me. I didn't 'do' coffee. But he came in and we had a cup of coffee. I found myself spending 40 minutes chatting about nothing with a neighbour, who I had very little in common with, which is a ridiculous thing to do when you're trying to build a big business and have only six months to get to a five-figure income. Time was precious – I wish in those early weeks that I'd realised just how precious. I should have said 'no' a lot more often. It would have moved me a lot more quickly towards my goals.

There were many other people distractions. It took me a little while to realise that you have to deal with them and become completely ruthless with your time. This is more important in the formative stages of business than any other. You can't afford to get distracted with the wrong things or by the wrong people – but I allowed myself to be knocked off course so many times in those first few months.

Growing up Fast

I made loads of mistakes, not least of which was in my marketing. I've already confessed to the brochure that I should have strangled at birth, but didn't. I thought it was fantastic but no one ever read or even looked at it. People don't read brochures because everyone is busy. They didn't care about my brochure; they cared about what was going on in their lives and their businesses. This was a big eye-opener for me. I was self-obsessed, always thinking about me, when I should have been 'customer obsessed' and thinking about them and how I could help them.

I wrote letters to businesses that I am so embarrassed about now. I've still got copies of them on my computer, and they're horrible. I thought of including one in this book as an example of how not to do things but it would be just too humiliating. Trust me – they were awful. Although one did get me a couple of customers, which I guess proves that the badly written sales letter that is mailed out will always outperform the beautifully written, perfectly crafted sales letter that never gets sent. There's a lesson in there somewhere!

I had to cold call businesses, which I'd never done before. I had had call centres full of hundreds of people doing that for me, but I'd never done it myself. It took all my self-discipline to knuckle down and force myself to dial those numbers. It was difficult. I wasn't very good at it in the beginning, but I got better – and I did get clients.

I had to confront that fear every Monday morning. Somehow I managed it. I had to because everything was on the line. I had to get on the phone, fill my calendar with appointments, go out and see potential clients, sell what I did and persuade business owners to let me work with them to make their business grow bigger and better.

This was another huge eye-opener for me – I was so naive in those early months! I had been quite fortunate for the previous 10 years at Barclays, the time at Caudwell and all my time at CPP where I had been surrounded by successful people who were very driven, very ambitious and hungry for success. I assumed everyone in business was like that. But they're not. As I went out and started meeting these small business owners, often what they had were quite good businesses with huge amounts of untapped potential. But they had no appetite or drive to do anything to improve their results and enhance their situation. They had no drive.

I was stunned at the reluctance of so many small business owners to do simple things that would dramatically improve their business and make them wealthy. They just weren't interested. I learnt that lots of people really like being in their comfort zone. They love the status quo.

This was in 2003, a time when the Internet was well established but most local business owners didn't yet have websites. They were convinced the web was a passing fad. There was so much I could do to help them. But so many weren't interested, and it wasn't just because my marketing was rubbish! It ran much deeper than that. They weren't prepared to do the few simple things that would make them much more profitable.

During the first half of 2003, I came to realise what the real world is actually like. It was difficult to get clients – much harder than I thought it would be – but I needed to get them on board. The target I'd set myself was that I needed 10 clients paying me £2,000 a month by the end of the summer. That's what I set out to achieve. I'd planned to get those 10 customers in the first six months, but it didn't happen like that.

At the end of four months, I had two clients, but I had done a lot of learning. In my quest for cash I began taking on some smaller clients – mainly people I met at local networking events. Some businesses couldn't afford the £2,000 per month, but they could afford a few hundred pounds, and I thought that would help boost my cash flow. Another massive mistake.

Who's Needy?

What I found is that there was a reason these people couldn't afford it: many of them had a horrible attitude and poor work ethic. These business were paying me less money but were asking more of me and being more demanding of my time *and* were the ones that were the most reluctant to implement the stuff I was doing for them. This was a big problem. They were too needy.

At the time, I was needy, too, because I was chasing the income. I had to replace that big six-figure salary, so I would say to myself that I better take this £500 a month. I remember thinking that it was better than nothing and it went towards a

Botty's Rule No. 2
Who you hang around with matters. A lot.

I used to play a lot of golf when I was younger. What I found was that I always played better when I played with golfers who were better than me. Similarly, whenever I played with people who weren't as good as me, I never played to my best. It's a bit like that in business.

Local networking events can be incredibly useful. You meet people, forge relationships and help each other to develop and grow. However, there are some who go to every single networking event but who are not, by any definition, successful. They are stuck in their rut, and if you spend too much time with them, then you will become like them.

In short, if you mix with losers, you become a loser. If you spend time with super-successful business owners, then your chances of achieving the same increase dramatically.

I think it was the late, great Jim Rohn – an entrepreneur and motivational speaker – who first said that you become a combination of the five people you spend most time with. Make sure you're spending time with the right people. People that inspire you, that motivate you, that fuel your ambition and drive and who you can learn from. Being around such people can make a heck of a difference to your level of success.

I was at least 12 months too late in realising this, and it held me back a lot in those early months.

target – this was bad thinking. Them being needy and me being needy was not a good combination. It took me a few months to realise this and to start pulling away from it, but I should never have compromised in the first place.

Motivational Accountant

One other thing that happened in those early days was that I got myself an accountant. His name was Geoff. Geoff was recommended to me by a friend of mine. I had a couple of meetings with him. He set up the N5 business and knew all about my plans. He also knew that I had a little bit of cash for the family to live on for six months while I built the business up.

I remember going to a New Year's Eve party on 31 December 2002. Geoff was there with his wife. He didn't remember who I was until I introduced myself. He asked if I was having a good night. I told him I was having a great night and he said, 'Well, make the most of it while you still have some money,' which I thought was a very strange thing for my accountant to say to me, because what was implicit and clear from his comment was that he expected me to fail.

In many ways, it was a big driving factor for me. I thought, 'I'll show him …' It made me very determined to succeed, and I'll confess that I took a little bit of pleasure, five years later, when I moved N5 from his accountancy firm to a much bigger practice because the business had simply outgrown what he could do for us.

Quiz Machines? You Are Joking, Right?

I talked earlier about how I read the *Rich Dad Poor Dad* book on the train on the way home from that fateful meeting in

London with Hamish Ogston. What I now knew, having read the book, was that I had to get assets that would generate revenue for me.

Therefore, what I did was invest a big chunk of my six-month sink fund after seeing an ad in the *Sunday Times* for a company that supplied quiz machines where people could play *Who Wants To Be a Millionaire* or *The Weakest Link*. These machines would be placed in clubs and pubs.

They supplied the machines and also found the pubs and clubs to place them in. You paid them a chunk of money to buy the machines and then you split the take from the machines with the landlord. I went to meet with this company near Manchester. I drove up there and was completely taken in by their sales pitch. It was very slick and all sounded great.

I thought, 'Well, if I have 50 machines out there, and they're all taking in £50 a week, that's over a grand a week for me (with a 50:50 split with the landlord).' I felt that this was a good deal and so when the guy in Manchester rang up the very next day after I'd met him and said he was just at the end of my road and wanted to come and see me, I welcomed him in eagerly. Big mistake yet again! Looking back now, I can see why he did that. He struck while the iron was hot and relieved me of a sizeable five-figure cheque.

A week later, I got all the machines delivered. They were placed in pubs and clubs all over the Midlands. They were hundreds of miles apart. From Cheltenham to Nottingham and everywhere in between.

I decided I would allocate a day a month to go around to all these machines and collect the money and do the bit of maintenance required. That was going to be a nice little residual income for me. It was going to be an asset working for me just like Mr Kiyosaki said in his book, but the reality was very different. It was a big (and very expensive) lesson to learn.

I spent a lot of money on those machines, yet I knew nothing about the business at all. First, anyone who knows me is going to think it's funny because I don't go into pubs or clubs very often. It's not my scene. What happened is these quiz machines broke down; they got vandalised; landlords move on. Every other day I was getting a phone call and having to drive out to sort a machine. It had a big impact on my ability to build my main businesses, because I was maintaining this one, which, by the way, wasn't generating £50 a week per machine – far from it, it was much less than that.

There were some fun times with that business but they didn't make up for the commercial calamity that I had stumbled into. I had to hire a big lorry to go collect the machines. It was a big seven-and-a-half tonner and my sons, Cameron and Elliott, being seven and eight years old at the time, thought it was brilliant to be going in the lorry with Daddy. We had some quite fun times doing that, but as a business, it was a disaster.

It wasn't just the commercial inadequacies of the machines, it was the huge opportunity cost. All the time I spent in dingy backstreet pubs and clubs I wasn't growing my consultancy business.

I bit the bullet after about 10 months and managed to sell the machines for a massive loss, but I pulled so many lessons from that failure. High-maintenance businesses are not good ones to get involved in and businesses that you know nothing about are definitely not something to pursue. In addition, I'd made the decision to buy the machines. Sure I'd been well sold to, but I wasn't going to allow myself to be a victim. It was my decision. My fault. I had to take responsibility.

'There's no such thing as victims, only volunteers,' says Lee Milteer, entrepreneur and business coach, and author of *Success Is an Inside Job*. And she's right.

Property Magnate … Not!

About this same time, again on the back of reading *Rich Dad Poor Dad*, I thought I better get some property. I'd read some stuff in the *Sunday Times* about a company called Inside Track. They were offering training courses on how to become a property developer. I enquired about the course, which sounded quite good. They sent me some details, so I asked them to give me a ring.

I remember I'd taken Tabitha, who was only around three years old at the time, to Stratford-Upon-Avon for a day out. (Distraction alert!) I remember walking through Stratford with Tabitha in her buggy and getting this phone call from the people at Inside Track. They told me the cost of this course was £6,000 and I nearly fell over. I thought that was a ridiculous price for a three-day course.

They had a very good salesperson who explained that what I would learn in the course was so valuable that it was worth many times more than £6,000. They explained how the course had the potential to completely change my life and that they should actually be charging twice as much. I found myself completely taken in by this so I wrote a cheque and booked on the course – which was taking place in Marbella!

The course was run by a guy named Jim Moore, who owned the company. I actually learnt a lot about property, how and what to buy and what to do. What they were also very good at in this course was selling you properties so you could put into practice what you'd just learnt.

I resisted the temptation to buy anywhere in Spain, but I did buy a couple of properties in Nottingham, which all looked fantastic. I needed some assets that would pay me a rental and that was an asset with appreciating value, so it was clearly the right thing to do. Fortunately, I only bought two.

I've still got them, if that tells you anything, and they're still worth less today, seven years after I bought them, than what I paid – but at least I have got tenants.

Interestingly enough, Inside Track went into liquidation a couple of years ago with a huge amount of bad press.

At the end of the day, what I've known since the day I went out on my own is that I'm responsible for what happens in my business. I take responsibility for what I do. With the quiz machines, it would be easy for me to blame the guy who sold them to me, but at the end of the day I'm a big boy. I make my own decisions, and that was a wrong one. I took a loss on it and learnt from it. I don't regret spending the money on the Inside Track course; I learnt a lot with it. I'm not sure in hindsight I should have bought those properties, but it was my decision to buy them. Make sure you take responsibility for what you do in life, even when it goes wrong, because that's a characteristic of all super-successful people.

Both the quiz machines and the property investments are only small footnotes in my business career. Truth is that neither have made me any money and one of them cost me a heck of a lot – but both taught me valuable lessons, for which I'm grateful.

Stairlifts and Wheel Spinners

But while all of this was going on, N5 was booming, and after seven or eight months, I'd managed to get myself a good amount of clients. My monthly revenue was heading towards the £20,000 goal that I'd set for myself. I had hired an assistant, and it was all going quite well.

I had some interesting clients. A guy named John Elliott rang me up one day. He ran a company called Elliotts Stairlifts, which was based near Slough. I remember him saying that he'd built the business up to £2 million a year but also said, 'I know I'm going to cock it up unless I get some advice ...' So I met John at a Heathrow Airport hotel a couple of days later and actually did a lot with him over the next 12 months.

He had a sales team that was really exploiting him in lots of ways. They ruled the roost over him. He employed his wife, son and daughter in the business, all in the 'back office' and none of them generating revenue. They all had flashy company cars and he was generating a lot of income but his expenses and commissions to his salespeople meant he had pretty much no profit. He was working harder and harder to stand still – a classic case of that old business mantra: 'Turnover is vanity; profit is sanity'. It was a little bit like Wallace and Gromit on the train track. He was pedalling so hard to just lay the track moments before the train ran over it, just like Wallace and Gromit do in *The Wrong Trousers*.

It was an interesting experience working with John. He was a good guy and I liked him, but he wasn't prepared to make the tough decisions and that meant that there was nothing solid for him to build upon. He got a couple of unexpected tax bills, and it was all over. The business folded.

I had another client at that time, a computer company based in Nottingham. The guy who ran it was called Peter. Right from the beginning, Peter was very honest with me that his company had big cash flow problems. He had some great ideas, but he had the wrong people working

Botty's Rule No. 3
Residual income is a beautiful thing ...

... it improves every aspect of your life and business.
I wish I'd understood many years ago the real power of residual income. To be clear, residual income is when your customers pay you (normally on a monthly basis), regardless of the amount of work you actually do. So, for instance, if you are a carpet cleaner, the amount of income you can earn in a month is directly related to the number of carpets that you clean. However, if you're a franchisee of thebestof, then your monthly income is dependent on how many customers you have as members. Those customers pay you monthly, by direct debit, and that money comes in each month regardless of the amount of work you actually do in that month. Oh, sure, you do have to do work. There are things that you need to deliver to ensure that the relationship with your customer is nurtured and developed and that you get them more customers and help them to grow, but there's a big difference between that type of relationship and the one where, for instance, you're cleaning carpets to earn your cash. Make sense?

All my businesses except My Mag have a residual income element. It helps in so many ways. First of all, we don't have to start every month at zero. We know that there's a big chunk of cash coming in by direct debit on the seventh of the month, say. This makes it much easier to run your business; you can plan with a much higher level of certainty. There is no week-by-week stress around meeting payroll or overheads, etc.

The second benefit of residual income is that it helps create significant value in your business as a whole. We've sold several of our thebestof franchises at significant capital gain to the franchisee because what they built was a business with £10,000 or £15,000 of monthly contracted direct debit income coming in. It's very easy in that situation for someone to pay a six-figure sum for a business because they can see the money's all there.

There are opportunities in many businesses to introduce residual income streams, but it's rarely exploited, particularly by local businesses. I mentioned in the previous Botty's Rule about the swimming pool company that now offers a maintenance service. Effectively, what they've done is put in place a modest residual income which helps meet their overheads each month. It was a smart strategy, and it's kept the wolves from their door during the depths of the recession.

It's definitely worth having a good old think and perhaps a chat with someone who knows what they're talking about to see if you can establish a residual income stream in your business. When you do, it really can be life-changing.

with him. The calibre of his staff wasn't right to do what he wanted to do.

Then, one day while I was there, Peter very excitedly took delivery of four incredibly flash alloy wheels (complete with spinners!) for his Range Rover. He had just spent £4,000 on a set of wheels for a Range Rover, when his business wasn't liquid. I knew then that was time to get out.

Not all my clients were unsuccessful. I had a great time working with some fab businesses. One in particular stands out. It was a business called Phonebox. It's (still) run by a man named Nigel Harrison. He was a very impressive individual. I learnt a few things from him, including the fact that business can be fun. There was a great atmosphere and vibe in his office. He had huge respect from his staff and from his competitors and other players in the industry.

I knew a lot about that industry from my time at Caudwell, so I had a lot of fun with Nigel. We did some progressive marketing for him that helped his business thrive and flourish.

Another client that I had a lot of fun with was Noel Farrelly, who runs Index Fund Advisors in Sutton Coldfield. Noel approached me looking for help to find 50 millionaire clients for his high-end financial advice business. I wondered if one day I might meet his client criteria myself ...

I found it hard being a consultant. Typically, clients were slow to do what you wanted them to do. There was huge reliance on me to not only come up with the ideas but to implement them as well. It wasn't something that I particularly enjoyed.

I earned good money while I was doing it, but I wasn't getting the fulfilment I was looking for and all my money was linked to the work that I did and the hours that I worked. What I wanted to do was build a proper business whereby I would have some residual income, ongoing money coming in that wasn't dependent on my hours of work. I was very keen to find something that would deliver me residual income.

First Impressions Can Be (Very) Wrong

If I was going to develop the business and generate residual income, then I needed to expand and get some help. So I placed a job ad in the local paper, seeking a telephone salesperson.

A very eloquent lady rang me. Her diction was perfect and she sounded like the archetypal Middle Englander. Her name was Audrey and I had in my head a picture of a Hyacinth Bucket character, a posh middle-aged lady. The voice, the name – it was obvious. It just shows how wrong first impressions can be. She came to my house for an interview the following day.

I went downstairs to answer the knock at the door and there was a Naomi Campbell lookalike standing there. She was an incredibly stunning black lady. Immaculately dressed and with this amazing voice. I was completely gobsmacked. Audrey was brilliant. We got on like a house on fire and, boy, could she sell. She was magic on the phones. She led the sales push. She was a great worker, very committed.

We started getting loads of clients. Audrey drew them in and I did the work to keep them. We packaged it up and shipped it out. We made a great team.

I hired another guy named Jez. He was an amiable and friendly chap who gave a great interview, but he had an absolute rubbish work ethic. I couldn't get him to turn up to work on time – even when he set his own hours! When he was there, he was sagging off. He just didn't have the drive that Audrey or I had. If you can believe it, I sacked Jez three times, twice more than I should have done. Why I took him back twice, I'll never know.

At the end of my first year in business, I had an income stream. While it hadn't been at all neat and tidy and I'd made a lot of mistakes along the way, I was turning over a five-figure sum each month, we were profitable and I still had a little bit of my cash reserve left.

I was a bone fide business owner and entrepreneur. I'd survived that very important first year and I was on my way …

CHAPTER 3
MY MAG LAUNCH

When I started N5, my wife, Sue, was incredibly supportive. At that point, she'd been a full-time mum for seven years. Sue was a languages graduate (she speaks fluent Russian and French and is conversational in four other languages as well). We'd met while working at Barclays. Like me, she had been a graduate entrant onto the fast-track Management Development programme and her last job before maternity leave (from which she never returned!) was in the bank's legal department. She hadn't worked outside the home because she was looking after our two boys Cameron and Elliott and then our daughter Tabitha, who was only two when I started the business.

Since I'd left my (very) well-paid employed position and set up on my own, Sue was keen to help out with the family finances. We knew we needed to earn a lot of money to maintain our lifestyle, and she wanted to do something to help towards that, so she started to look for a job.

All the jobs she could find were either those that paid her what she thought she was worth and had no flexibility around the children or else they were jobs that had flexibility, but didn't pay her what she felt she was worth. She was caught in a trap that I know is familiar to many parents, especially mums. Sue wrestled with her conundrum for a few months and then, one day in March 2003, I came downstairs from the office in early evening and Sue announced that she knew what she wanted to do.

'I'm going to launch a magazine for our village,' she informed me.

Well, I just humoured her.

'Yes, dear, of course you are,' I said to my eternal shame and embarrassment.

'No no, it'll work really well,' she explained. 'I'm going to do a little magazine and businesses will advertise in it, and I can put everything that's going on in the village in it. We can tie it in with the school, the church, scout groups and everyone will love it because there are all these people moving into the area and no one knows about the village or where to go for anything.'

Her enthusiasm was wonderful and I hadn't the heart to burst her bubble. I just went along with it, but deep down I felt sure this would end in disappointment. I couldn't have been more wrong.

Sue was incredibly enthused by the thought of setting up her own magazine and running her own business. My problem was that I felt she was completely ill-equipped to make it a success. She'd never sold anything in her life. She hadn't even met a computer at that point because they hadn't arrived in the workplace before she'd left work to raise our family, so I felt sure that there was no way this was ever going to work.

Sue had no such doubts, and she is a very formidable lady. For lots of reasons I'm very lucky to have her as my wife and what Sue accomplished over the following six weeks was, by any standard, quite remarkable.

The following morning she left to take the boys to school with Tabitha in her car seat in the back, and in the queue of traffic on the way to school, she found herself sitting behind a locksmith's van. It was a company called Key Edge, with a local phone number on the truck. Sue found a pen while in the traffic jam and jotted down the phone number on the van. She dropped off the boys at school and noticed that Tabitha had fallen asleep in her car seat. She seized the moment, took a deep breath and rang the locksmith on her mobile phone from the school car park.

She told him she was doing a magazine for Dickens Heath, our village. She explained that she needed a local locksmith in the magazine, because no one in the village knew where to go for a locksmith when they needed one and that the magazine would be perfect for him and she felt sure that he would love to feature in her magazine. He was clearly taken by her enthusiasm, and after a fairly short conversation he agreed it was a great idea to advertise in the magazine and placed his order.

Humble Pie – Big Slice …

Sue came rushing home to tell me the news about having her first customer. I was pleased for her, obviously, and, if I'm honest, a bit surprised. Anyway, later that afternoon, I had to eat a huge slice of humble pie. It was a diet I had to get used to over the coming weeks.

I was working in the house on my own when there was a knock on the door. I answered it and I was asked if this was the Dickens Heath Directory. The guy at the door explained that he was bringing his cheque for Sue along with the ad. I was completely stunned. He paid £180 – in advance – for three months' advertising! Sue was in business and, although we didn't know it at the time, our destiny in business had just been changed for ever.

In many ways, I owe a lot to the local locksmith in Dickens Heath. Who knows what would have happened if he'd said

Botty's Rule No. 4
Attitude is everything ...

... attitude is the foundation of everything.
This is a quote from Jeffrey Gitomer, an American who's a real master of selling. In *The Little Gold Book of Yes! Attitude*, Jeffrey articulates the importance of attitude to success in business and in life.

There's a great vibe in our offices at N5. Of course, things go wrong occasionally, but we're an incredibly 'can do' bunch. No one is allowed to be down for more than a few minutes and we all smile. It's not forced; it happens naturally because everyone in N5 has the right attitude. Give me the right attitude over skills or experience, because those I can teach, but attitude is much harder to learn. With it, however, you can build businesses bloody fast, and have fun on the way.

You do have to work at having a great attitude because we all take knock-backs occasionally and despite what people say, I don't believe you were born with your attitude. (Imagine the scene in the maternity ward, 'Congratulations, Mrs Smith, it's a baby boy ... the bad news is, he's a negative one!' It wouldn't happen, would it?)

This is particularly important if you're a business owner. It's lonely and bad things do happen. Regularly. You'd better make sure you've got the right support system in place and the right people around you to help get you back up when you take a knock, and you have to get back up quickly. You can't fester in self-pity or negativity for days, not if you're running your own business. My Entrepreneurs' Circle can help you with your attitude. Full details are at **www.nigelbotterill.com/bookoffer**.

ATTITUDE

no to Sue's phone call. It could have put her off the whole magazine project and everything would be different, but he didn't. He said yes, and she was off to a flying start.

There is a real lesson here in the importance of taking action. I'm full of admiration for Sue making that call from the school car park. It would have been really easy for her to procrastinate. All she had was an idea, a vision. She had no business cards, no product, no brochure, nothing. Yet she made that call and got her first customer and so many business owners can learn from that. So many business owners are 'world class' at getting ready. They find reason after reason to keep on getting ready and avoid taking their idea or business 'out there', Sue didn't. She took action and got the success she deserved.

What got Sue's business rolling was making that phone call from the school car park. She had loads of reasons not to make that call, but she did, and it got her started.

After her first initial success Sue became completely obsessed with her magazine. For the next five weeks, every spare moment, when she wasn't busy with the children, was spent on the magazine.

She had a system to collect leads. She would go through local newspapers and clip out ads from businesses. As she drove by shops or passed a van, say, she'd write information down. Every potential advertiser was given their own sheet of pink paper. At the end of that first month, she had 180 sheets of pink paper, because she'd contacted 180 local businesses asking them to advertise. Sixty of those businesses agreed to become her customers, and they were featured in her first magazine.

When Sue sent her first magazine off to print, which she did after only four weeks of selling it, she made £1,785 profit.

A couple of weeks in, even I could now see that this was a worthwhile thing for her to be doing, so I helped her learn some new skills on the computer. I helped her publish the magazine properly, and I insisted that she put my office phone number on the magazine rather than the home number so Audrey or I could answer calls for her.

Part-Time Publisher, Full-Time Mum

One very interesting thing in that first month was that businesses paid Sue upfront for their ads. Now, that's *not* normal in advertising, but Sue didn't know that. Normally businesses would be invoiced after the magazine had gone to print and then they'd pay 30 days after that. But most of Sue's customers paid her upfront ... because she asked them to. She was wonderfully naive – and devastatingly effective as a result. Sue didn't know what 'the norm' was, so she did what she thought was sensible. And when she asked people for their cheque, the vast majority gave it to her. Big lesson. Huge.

You see, you don't have to follow industry norms. I'll talk about this again in a later chapter – about how, in any industry or sector, the majority of people are wrong about pretty much everything. I had learnt that with Caudwell and Hamish Ogston and here was Sue putting it into practice at a very low level.

Sue was very cash positive from day one – literally, because the locksmith paid her £180 before she had incurred a penny of cost of any kind. Her first magazine was printed and the whole family helped with distribution. Her mum and dad helped. My mum and dad came down from Leeds to help. (This later became a regular monthly event and my dad claimed at one point that he was the oldest paperboy in the country!) The children got involved, and between us, we put all the magazines, 2,000 of them, out over a two-day weekend. We delivered them free through doors in our little village. Then something incredible happened …

On Monday morning, the phone started ringing in the office with all these home-based businesses. They were people that lived in Dickens Heath enquiring about advertising in the Dickens Heath Directory. They'd received their copy of the magazine through their letterbox at the weekend, and now they wanted their business to feature in the next edition. We had 15 phone calls in two days from new advertisers who wanted to be in Sue's magazine. Audrey and I took messages and passed them on to Sue, and she closed the sales.

Sue's second edition made £2,700 profit, so she was well and truly off and running and contributing significantly to the family coffers. She didn't need a job at all. She had her own publishing business with all the flexibility she needed and earnings that, when you worked out the hourly rate, were way ahead of anything she would have got as an employee.

Sue developed the magazine in a number of ways. She got the magazines distributed in the show homes of one or two house builders in the area because, of course, the magazine was a great asset to people who were buying new homes. She started to do a restaurant review in the magazine. We'd go along, and she would take her notepad and her camera, and she'd talk to the owner and write a review on the restaurant, which was all printed in the magazine. The owners always gave us the meal for free. Always.

Most importantly, Sue ran the magazine around being a great mum. She never compromised with the children and her work fitted in around them. One time she went into a big lawnmower business called Breakwells. It was a sizeable operation, with showrooms and workshops, and it had been around for over 80 years. Sue had an appointment with them; she thought she was going just to pick up an advert, so she popped in on the way back from Tabitha's Rhythm Time class. When she got there, the receptionist asked her to wait and then told her that Mr Breakwell, the Managing Director, was ready for her. She was shown into this very sumptuous wood-panelled office. Very grand, it was.

Now, Tabitha was two at the time. It was spring and she was sucking on a big ice lolly. Sue hadn't even brought in her changing bag with all her wipes and other kiddy paraphernalia, as she thought she was only going to be a couple of minutes. But she was shown up to this very smart office and as the Managing Director started to talk with Sue about the magazine, Tabitha's lolly was dripping and leaking all over this guy's carpet and desk. Sue was mortified but Mr Breakwell was completely fascinated with her business and how the magazine was working. He signed a 12-month contract for advertising and even cleaned up the sticky mess himself. This goes to show that you don't have to be 'corporate' to succeed in a corporate environment, and you can take your two-year-old on sales calls if you're positioned properly.

Sue was very non-corporate and non-traditional. Most people will tell you that you can't go selling adverts to big companies when you have a two-year-old in tow sucking an ice lolly, but you can if you have the right attitude and the right approach, and Sue had both. Having Tabitha with her made Sue even more 'real' to these local businesses, who loved the fact that a local resident was shouting about them to everyone in the village. Genius.

Sue found it was much better to sell packages in order to get businesses to commit for three, six or 12 months because that reduced her workload and also boosted her cash flow. Although she discounted the packages, businesses would pay her upfront – that was her deal. What she found was that in 15–20 hours a month, she was selling and producing the magazine, which was generating between £2,500 and £3,000 a month profit.

What was really interesting was that one year in, Sue did a piece of work one day where she laid out all those pink pieces of paper she had collected from that very first edition. There were those 180 businesses, and what was fascinating was that by the end of her first year, all except one of them had advertised in the magazine at some point during the year. So, even though only 60 had come in the first month, 179 of them had placed adverts in that first year. And there's another lesson.

Sue kept in touch with all those businesses. She made sure that every one of them received a copy of her magazine every month, so they would see it growing. She would pop in to see them so they could see she was serious. They heard from her regularly; they saw that she was delivering on what she had promised and, over 12 months, they all came aboard.

Info Product

I'm very proud of Sue and what she did in that first 12 months of the Dickens Heath Directory. She didn't do things because she had lots of training in sales and marketing – far from it. She just did what she thought was sensible and what was right, and she had the discipline and work ethic to do it rigorously and consistently. She built a really brilliant business.

After a few months of publishing the Dickens Heath Directory, people started asking Sue if she could help them set up their own local magazines. This was an interesting idea, but it seemed like a lot of work. Sue was non-committal. Then I met an American guy named Martin Howey. I got to know him quite well, and he was very impressed with Sue's magazine.

He felt there was an Info Product in her idea, but at that time, I'd never heard of the words 'Info Product'. I found out

Botty's Rule No. 5
Deadlines get stuff done.

This is the second most valuable tool that I've used to build my business over the last seven or eight years. In particular, I ask myself this question:

If I had to do X by Y, or else I would die, could I get it done?

If you had to get 20 testimonials for your business by next Monday or you died, could you do it? The answer will, I'm sure, be 'Yes'. You've now removed any doubt or questions about whether it can be done. What you then have to do is prioritise and that's where our deadlines come in. So we ask ourselves that question, get to a 'Yes' answer and then prioritise it alongside other things and give it a deadline.

That's how we get things done. In the beginning, it was only me that used to use this phrase, but now I take a lot of pleasure from hearing it being used around my business. It's a really neat tool.

Other ways we use deadlines, for instance, is to go public whenever we've got some big projects to deliver, and announce to the world (to our customers or our franchisees, say) that this new thing is going to come on this date.

When I came back from that conference in America, I gave myself a five-week deadline to launch My Mag. If I hadn't, it might never have happened.

Deadlines keep everybody focused on getting things delivered and implemented, and that's the key.

that it's a way you package information and teach people how to do things so it has a value. The idea sat in my head and I pondered it.

Around the same time I received an email from a man named Yanik Silver. I had bought an eBook that Yanik had produced called *Instant Sales Letters*. It had helped me with my consultancy work.

A few weeks after I bought the book, I got an email from Yanik inviting me to his thirtieth birthday bash in Orlando, Florida. I thought, what a nice thing to do. I'd never met this guy and here he was inviting me to his birthday bash. Basically, Yanik was putting on this big event in Orlando where he had all these famous speakers (that I'd never heard of), but it

Botty's Rule No. 6
Good is good enough.

Perfection in business is vastly overrated …

My good friend, Bill Glazer, taught me that 'good is good enough'. For three years, I was part of Bill's Mastermind Group and I used to fly out to the States three times a year and sit round a boardroom table with Bill and a dozen other switched-on entrepreneurs. Those sessions were hugely helpful to me in the development and growth of my business. They were pivotal in my education as an entrepreneur and inspirational every time I went.

So many people in business strive for perfection, but it really isn't necessary (I accept that there are some exceptions to this, but they are exceptions, and there aren't that many of them. So, don't let yourself off the hook that easily!) It's the classic implementation of the 80:20 rule and we've made a habit of launching products and services that are 80% perfect but which become very profitable very quickly. In some cases, we hone them and perfect them over time. In other cases, we don't even need to bother doing that because commercially it's just not necessary.

I remember one of the comments around the table at one of those Mastermind meetings once was that 'The badly written, poorly crafted sales letter that is mailed out will always outperform the beautifully written, perfectly crafted sales letter that never gets sent', and that for me personifies this rule.

Much better to take action, albeit not completely perfect action, than to do nothing and remain stationary.

sounded quite interesting so I had to decide if I wanted to spend the £500 for airfare and the cost of staying in a hotel for a couple of nights.

I was very undecided as to whether or not I should go. I remember talking to my dad on the phone and he said to me, 'Nige, you're in business on your own now, you've got a lot to learn. How will you learn new things if you don't go when you have the opportunity? I think you should get on that plane.'

Sue said the same thing, so I spent the £500, bought my flight and went off to Orlando. That trip completely changed my life.

At the event, I met people like Dan Kennedy, Bill Glazer, Tom Antion, Corey Rudl and many others who subsequently were very influential to me. At that event, what I absolutely realised is that what Martin Howey had said was right, that there was an Info Product with Sue's magazine.

Five weeks after attending Yanik's birthday bash, Sue and I launched My Mag. It was a comprehensive package that taught people everything they needed to know to set up, launch, market, produce and administer their own local community magazine. We gave them tools and templates, training and tips. Everything.

I learnt there and then that setting deadlines is the way to get things done. I came back, looked at the calendar, decided that we'll launch on one particular day and we did.

It was difficult, but by having a deadline, we got there and delivered it.

At this point I also learnt that 'good is good enough'. Up until then, I'd been something of a perfectionist, and perfection is vastly overrated in business. In my experience, perfection is hardly ever worth the time or the cost.

People spend a lot of time chasing perfection, when they could be doing much more valuable things. We got My Mag out there after four weeks. I placed some classified ads in parenting magazines. I got a few phone calls, and we made the first sale before the My Mag pack was finished, which was an eye-opener because I remember we had a holiday booked.

I remember sitting on a towel by a swimming pool in St Lucia writing the final chapters of the My Mag Info Product. I sold the My Mag product for £1,700, which I initially thought was ridiculous for what was essentially a box of binders and CDs that cost me about £50. I made the mistake that most business owners make in thinking price should be based on cost. It shouldn't. Price should be based on value. My Mag helped people set up their own publishing business that could generate £2,000+ per month in profit. That's a lot of value! Fortunately, by learning from others, I learnt about pricing, made some sales at the £1,700 level and we were up and away.

Pay-per-Click Pioneer

People started buying it. Every time someone bought it, I reinvested all the money from the sales into more advertising. The more I advertised, the more people started to buy. I began getting testimonials, so I decided to put it on a website. I got a local web guy, John Harper, to help me with this. John was in his early fifties and was providing a local web design service to businesses in and around Solihull.

I then started spending money on pay-per-click (Google AdWords), which, in the spring of 2004, was quite a new thing. I remember during that time, John Harper was in my office one day and he happened to see my statements from Google. I'd spent £2,000 the previous week on pay-per-click, and he was quick to tell me that I was spending way too much money on Google advertising and that he could save me a fortune.

I realised that he completely didn't get it. I wanted to spend a lot *more* money with Google, because with every £1 I was spending on pay-per-click I was getting £8 or £9 back in sales. On that basis, my aim was to spend as much as I could, because then I'd get even more back.

His driver, on the other hand, and that of so many other people in small businesses, is to manage cost. He had no concept of ROI (return on investment). I had the blessing of understanding the difference between cost and value, because every time I gave Google £1, I was getting £9 back. That was brilliant and I wanted to spend more and more with Google, which is just what I did that summer – despite John's well-intentioned attempts to stop me!

Every time I spent more money, I'd make more sales. By the middle of that summer, the revenue from My Mag was starting to equal the revenue from my consultancy business.

The First Profitable Mistake …

One of the big mistakes that Sue and I made with My Mag was also one of the best things we never did. Let me explain …

We'd launched this as an Info Product so there was no ongoing revenue for us.

People bought a My Mag Pack, and they could then do what they wanted with it, but there was no back-end revenue stream for us. No money came in subsequently from these people. We sold them the rights to a postcode area and once we sold an area, we couldn't sell it again. There was no on going licence fee or profit share. They bought the box, and that was it.

Many people told us that this was a big mistake. They said we should be charging ongoing fees, or forcing people to print with a specific printer who would pay us a cut, but actually, that combination of giving people exclusivity on their postcode area and not tying them to any ongoing obligations was one of the reasons why My Mag was so phenomenally successful. You see, people loved the fact that there were no ongoing obligations – and that we wouldn't sell to anyone else on their patch. Ultimately it meant that My Mag appealed to a wider audience, and we sold a lot more as a result.

It's another big lesson that is very, very clear with hindsight: do what's right for your customers, and you'll do just fine.

The Power of the Press

In the summer of 2004, shortly after we had put the website up, I took a phone call from a lady who introduced herself to me as Clare McVey. She told me she'd been commissioned by the editor of *Red* magazine (one of the leading women's glossy magazines in the UK) to write an article about women who were working part time from home.

She'd found Sue on the website – thanks to our pay-per-click advertising. She thought Sue would make a great subject for this article and she explained that she'd like to interview Sue and include her in the feature. This was not a difficult decision to say yes to!

Clare spoke at length with Sue, and a photo shoot was organised for late July. The article didn't appear until the beginning of November, coming out in the December 2004 issue. The first Monday morning after that magazine hit news-stands, our phone lines went absolutely berserk.

We got incredibly lucky. There was a massive lesson for me about the power of the media and the press, because that article generated well over £250,000 worth of sales for us in the space of about six weeks. It was a complete game changer, where all of a sudden we had this really big business. It was quite extraordinary.

It was a crazy time. I got anybody who could talk to come to the office just to answer the phone, because every time we answered the phone, we had people paying us £3,000 for the My Mag Pack – yes, I had put the price up!

We got lucky, and I think you need a bit of good fortune to succeed in business. I won't pretend that we were really smart and clever about all of this. But we did a few things right to generate that luck. For instance, we'd put the website out there and were spending on pay-per-click, which is how Clare McVey, found us in the first place, but the bottom line is that article made a huge difference to our fledgling business.

What was interesting is that quite a few months after the article was published, we received another call from Clare McVey who explained that she was now expecting her first child and didn't want to work in London any more, so she wanted to know if she could buy a My Mag Pack.

There was no way I was going to let her buy one. I gave her one for free and included three postcode areas as well. It was the least we could do. Clare is, to this day, one of our most successful My Maggers. Her magazines in Gloucestershire flourish and she joins people like Malcolm Hewitt, Yanik Silver and Bill Glazer as one of the very key individuals who has helped us to shape our business and has played a big part in our success. Thank you, Clare, I'm ever so glad you rang!

International Marketer of the Year

The Monday morning that the *Red* article hit the streets was the morning I came back from my second trip to America. At Yanik's event earlier in the year, I had met Bill Glazer who had persuaded me to subscribe to the Glazer-Kennedy Insider Circle. The organisation had an annual conference every November. That year it was in Cleveland, so I went along. It was quite a modest affair, very different to the huge extravaganzas that they run now (and which I still attend each year). There were about 300 people at the event in 2004.

On the last day, they had a contest whereby people could enter to compete to be crowned 'Info Marketer of the Year'. I thought I would have a go at this. I'd done no preparation at all, but entered while I was there. I was the only Brit in the room; everyone else was American.

I hadn't quite realised how much Americans love the British accent, so I stood up on stage and told this quite self-deprecating story about My Mag and how we'd launched it after the Yanik Silver birthday bash.

I talked about all the mistakes we'd made. I explained how every month I put the price up, so I sold it at £1,700 the first month and then upped it to £1,800 and then £2,000 and so on, which actually became an interesting sales tool because it made people take action. They had to buy before the end of the month or the price went up. Every time we put the price up, we sold more units.

It went up by an average of £100 a month for two years until it settled at £3,500, which is where we capped it. It's still that price today, and we still sell My Mag Packs every month. It's a brilliant product with an outstanding track record and hundreds and hundreds of successful publishers.

I had only 10 minutes to tell my story at the event in Cleveland, but the Americans loved it. The Marketer of the Year title was decided by a vote of all the people in the audience, and I was genuinely quite stunned when it was announced that I had won.

I arrived back in the UK triumphant, clutching this quite ridiculous five-foot-high trophy. I arrived back, jetlagged, into the frenzy that was all these phones ringing on the back of the *Red* magazine article. It really felt like we'd reached a high.

Sue and I had just celebrated our second anniversary in business – it was exactly two years since that fateful meeting with Hamish Ogston – and we now had a successful business. We were doing big numbers and were getting recognition and winning awards.

As I sat on the plane coming back from Cleveland, I reflected on where we were. What was making us successful was the fact that we'd become marketers, not doers, of our business model. I'd spent that year, 2004, marketing the My Mag Pack, and my single-minded focus on marketing the

Botty's Rule No. 7
Become a 'marketer' *not* a doer.

To build a big business, the business owner has to become a 'marketer' of their thing, not a 'doer' of their thing.

This is something that the great Dan Kennedy (**www.DanKennedy.com**) taught me (along with quite a few other things that I talk about in this book).

Most business owners are very much *doers* of whatever it is that they do. My friend Julie is a florist. Julie loves creating beautiful things with flowers – it's what she gets her pleasure and fulfilment from – but she knows that in making the conscious decision to be a *doer* of floristry, she is inhibiting the growth of her business.

In contrast, my friend David Costa is also a florist. The difference is David sees himself as a marketer of floristry services. What he is focused on is finding new customers and looking after the ones that he's got. That's why he's one of Interflora's top three florists in the whole of the UK – he sees himself as a marketer of floristry services: he spends his time marketing his business and thinking about how he can better market his business.

If you want to build a super-successful business, then you have to get focused for very large chunks of time on the marketing and that starts with how you see your role.

Are you a *marketer* or a *doer*? It matters.

There's no way my business would have grown like it has if I hadn't understood this *and* made the shift.

business had been key to our success. It helped, of course, that My Mag was such a good product and that so many people were having great success with it but, ultimately, it was because we were getting better and better at marketing it that our sales were growing so fast.

To get a big breakthrough in business, what you have to do is change your thinking. I had changed from being a 'paid by the hour' consultant to being a marketer of an Info Product – My Mag – and as long as I focused on the marketing, I could keep growing the business and growing our profits. I resolved, on that flight from Cleveland back to England, to always be a 'marketer' of what we did – and never to be a 'doer' of what we did because I knew that if we stuck to that, we had the potential to build something very big and very special that would affect not just our lives but potentially thousands of other lives as well.

This theme is something that I'll carry forward into the next chapter, because the N5 story was about to ramp up still further …

CHAPTER 4
SACK THE CLIENTS ...
WE'VE GOT A REAL
BUSINESS HERE

As I mentioned in the previous chapter, in the summer of 2004 My Mag started to generate as much revenue in a month as my consultancy business. The first month that happened was in July 2004. We had the website up and generated £25,000 in My Mag sales that month, and we had just under £20,000 of consultancy income.

There were only four of us running things: me, Sue, Audrey and Jez, so we were very profitable. My Mag was generating more money, but there was a lot more work involved with my consultancy clients. We started to develop and experiment with the website for My Mag, and I realised that it was a lot of fun marketing the product. It's much more exciting making money for yourself than it is for your clients!

What I was very concerned about was that we had this big opportunity here with My Mag, and I wondered how big it could actually get. I started to wonder how I could give My Mag the time and attention it deserved while still maintaining all these consultancy clients. I was already working 12–14 hours every day, including weekends, but I needed to find the capacity from somewhere to do more work marketing and selling My Mag. I began by investing a bit of our monthly income and brought a bookkeeper on board.

The story of how she came on board is quite an interesting one. I had contacted a local temp agency (Plum Personnel in Solihull – they're fab and we still use them for all our temporary staff requirements) because I needed some help putting all the My Mag Packs together. We needed someone to physically put things in binders and make up the packs to send out because we were selling so many of them. They sent me a lady called Brenda Brown who was in her mid-fifties at the time. One day, Brenda was in my spare bedroom making these boxes up, and I started chatting to her. It turned out that Brenda was a qualified bookkeeper.

Long story short, as well as for packing boxes, I also employed Brenda as my bookkeeper. She still keeps all our books today, although she no longer packs boxes! She's our Finance Manager at N5 and one of my most valued employees. Having someone else to do the bookkeeping took one piece of work away from me, but I still had all these clients to look after. I wanted to develop My Mag, so I was getting torn as to what I really should be doing. I was doing a lot of reading at this time and from the stuff I was reading, I knew that as it was my business, what happened in it was 100% my responsibility. (Remember Botty's Rule No. 1!)

The Free Event that Cost Me £10,000

It had never been part of the plan to develop an info-marketing business, but that's what we had done. The first time I had a big change and adaptation in my business was when we started to market the consultancy service as fixed-price marketing rather than just one-to-one consultancy. We were at the crossroads of another big change because we had a business that was hugely profitable and had huge potential with My Mag.

Remember that every month the price went up by £100, so we were making a lot of money. Our customers were happy because the value they were getting from My Mag was a business that earned them £1,500–£3,000 pcr month profit, so our price (of £2,000 and rising) represented great value for them. But the pack only cost us £50 (including shipping) to put together, which made it so profitable. I just felt I had to find out how big this could become if I gave it focus.

Although Yanik's birthday bash in Orlando was a free event to attend, when I was there I spent about £10,000. I met all these amazing people who were hugely inspirational, and I bought all their stuff.

I bought Michael Cage's teleseminar programme. I joined Bill Glazer's Mastermind Group. I learnt from John Reese, Corey Rudl and Perry Marshall, among others, and bought their material. I was studying and learning all this stuff. It was a massive eye-opener for me as to what was possible, and what I could do.

Around that same time, Dan Kennedy launched his Renegade Millionaire programme, on which I also spent a couple of thousand pounds.

I remember ringing up Dan's office asking if they could ship it to me quickly because I was going on holiday to France in August and wanted to take it with me to study while on holiday. (There's probably a lesson in that somewhere as well.)

Campsite Learning in France

We went to the Vendée in western France and stayed at a beautiful campsite. I'd agreed with Sue that I would get 90 minutes each day where I could sit and listen to the CDs from Dan

Botty's Rule No. 8
To get high income, just get more done …

High-income businesses are just better at implementation. There's no two ways about it: if you want to build your business and be more successful, you've got to find a way to get more stuff done. Implementation is key.

You can have the greatest plans in the world, but if you're not implementing them effectively, then you're not making things happen.

Many business owners I meet are world class at getting ready. They spend months building their new project to perfection, and they never get it out there.

Others make long lists of things that they really want to do. They're sincere about it, but inevitably daily life takes over and few things get crossed off the list.

One of the differences between super-successful business owners and the rest is the amount of things that we're able to get done. It just comes down to focus and keeping track of what we've achieved this week, not what we are working on. There's a big difference.

Try to find one hour of uninterrupted time every day when you can work 'on' your business and you'll begin to make rapid progress. (If you're really so busy working 'in' your business that you can't find an hour each day, then you'd better set your alarm and get up one hour earlier.) Recognise that without dedicated focused chunks of time to get things done, you'll never implement your plans as well as the best … and therefore you'll never join us!

Kennedy's Renegade Millionaire programme. It was a series of interviews between Dan Kennedy and Lee Milteer. I made copious notes and the lessons I learnt from these interviews were immense, but the most striking one was the importance of focus in your business.

At this point I'd just got rid of the quiz machines, but I was really split in so many different directions, especially with all these consultancy clients, so I made the decision on that holiday in France to sack all the clients in my consultancy business and give My Mag a proper chance.

That's what I resolved to do, and when I came back, in a very nice way, I sacked all my clients. It took me two weeks, and I found other people to work with them. It wasn't quite as bold and brave as it sounds. I knew how to get new clients, so if My Mag crashed and burnt, I could always go back to what I'd been doing.

One thing that's important to mention about My Mag is that it was not a new idea. There have been little community and parish magazines for as long as there have been printing presses. It wasn't that we had a new idea, but what we were doing very well at that point was implementing that idea in a fresh and exciting way.

We were marketing My Mag extremely effectively, which is another big learning point. I was sufficiently self-aware to understand that it's not about the idea, it's the implementation that determines your success in business. I was absolutely determined that we were going to implement our product well. We weren't going to cock it up, and we were going to build something really big.

Guarantees

We tried a number of different things during that summer. We decided to put a guarantee on My Mag. We created a seven-day money-back guarantee that said if you get this pack and don't like it, you can send it back within seven days.

What a disaster that was.

Here was another big lesson for me. I was learning about the psychology of buyers. What happened was people were getting completely seduced by the My Mag story. The true story was exciting, and we had loads of other people now replicating Sue's success.

Typically, the buyers of My Mag were people like Sue. They were mums with young kids who needed to earn an income but didn't go out to work. They wanted flexibility, but they needed the revenue. My Mag was perfect for that. So, they'd ring us up, we'd have a little chat and answer their questions, then they would decide to buy. We'd ship it out to them, the box would arrive, and then they'd see all this stuff. At the end of the day, this box had a lot of material in it that needed to be read and put into action in order build your (very) profitable local business.

They would see that you have to work hard. Buying the box doesn't, on its own, get you a business that makes you £2,000 a month – you have to do the work. What was happening is that people were opening the box, seeing all that stuff, understanding what they needed to do and thinking, 'Oh, what have I done? I've spent £3,000 on this, and now I have all this work to do. I've got a seven-day guarantee. Thank goodness for that! I'll send it back.' I was learning about the psychology of buyer's remorse.

Since the seven-day guarantee only lasted seven days, a lot of packs came back. I decided that wasn't the right thing to do. People don't like doing work, so a seven-day guarantee is the wrong thing to do, because people are focused on getting it back quickly because they only have seven days.

Whereas, if we gave them a longer guarantee period, six months, say, then they wouldn't be obsessed about the seven days. That way, they could concentrate on doing the work and making it happen.

We found that by having a longer guarantee (six months instead of seven days), we made more sales and a lot less people returned their packs. Interesting, huh?

Exhibitionist Tendencies

That summer, I found out there was a big franchise exhibition happening at the NEC in Birmingham in October and got excited about that because My Mag was like a franchise. I rang up and tried to book My Mag into the exhibition. When they found out that I wasn't a real franchise, because we didn't have a franchise agreement and there were no ongoing obligations, they said we couldn't exhibit.

I didn't want to take that no for an answer, so I kept going back and talking to the people who were organising the exhibition. I pestered and pestered. Finally, they accepted and allowed us to exhibit, even though we weren't technically a franchise. We went to the exhibition and, like so many things that we've done throughout the history of N5, we knew nothing about this. We didn't know what the established way to do things was, so we just went along.

Sue got a few of her friends to come, and we turned up in jeans and branded T-shirts with messages on the back. The people who were wearing them were women who were doing My Mag, so people could actually talk to them. We had no big corporate logos, stands or displays. We wallpapered our stand with newspaper, which looked a bit strange, to be honest, but it was quite eye-catching.

We had all these women in jeans and T-shirts, whereas every other stand that had women there had them in smart business suits. There were mainly men manning all the stands, all suited and booted in their shirts and ties. Our big banner said the prices started at £2,500, about £10,000 less than anything else at the exhibition. We were completely deluged. We stole the entire show. Our stand was overrun from the minute the show opened until it closed seven hours later.

We sold loads of My Mags on the back of this first exhibition. Dozens and dozens of them. We learnt a lot about how to run a good exhibition as well. We became good at capturing contact details. On Monday morning after the event, we followed up by ringing people who had visited the stand at the weekend. We made loads of sales from just following up people's initial enquiries.

Botty's Rule No. 9
Follow up, follow up, follow up ...

Super-successful businesses follow up with their prospects much more than ordinary businesses do.
We learnt this initially on the back of that first My Mag exhibition, but it's been reinforced many times since.

Lots of businesses never follow up with prospects after an exhibition or any kind of first enquiry. The majority only follow up once or twice. What I've learnt is that its takes seven, nine, 12, sometimes 26 communications and follow-ups for most people to make a final decision to purchase anyone's product or service.

Most businesses give up after one or two. Some are really proud that they have a five-step follow-up programme. Truth is, if you're giving up before 10, then you're almost certainly missing out ... big time.

We regularly make sales to people who first enquired over a year ago. The reason they buy is because we stayed in touch – we followed up.

You'll know this for yourself. There'll be times when you think about making a decision on something you're interested in but you never quite get around to it – and then it's that one thing you see in an email, brochure or that you hear on the phone that makes you decide to do it.

If you want to stay a small business for ever, then just make sure you never follow up more than two or three times with your customers and prospects!

We built our network to such a point that within three years we had over 1,200 My Maggers across the UK. It generated cash, it built traction, our reputation flourished on the back of it and we had lots of successful case studies. We were putting prices up every single month, which helped enormously in making sales. We got heavily into Google pay-per-click, being one of the first organisations to do that. For a couple years in 2004 and 2005, I, little ole' Nige in Solihull, England, was one of Google's top 50 clients in Europe on pay-per-click.

Although we were spending an awful lot of money with them, we got ahead of the game in that respect, and we did that because our eyes were open. We were willing to learn, and when we learnt new things, we implemented what we had discovered.

Winning that award in Cleveland in November 2004 was great, but guess what? I went back the following year and won it again – because of what we did in 2005.

Log Cabin or Long Commute?

At this point, we were recruiting people and growing a proper team. As usual, we made a lot of mistakes doing this. We hired some shocking people. Don't get me wrong: I've uncovered some complete superstars as well. One nightmare scenario developed when we brought someone on board who was quite a close friend of ours. It all went horribly wrong, spectacularly so. It caused a lot of anguish for them and pain for us.

We had other staff that stole from us and one tried to copy our ideas and set up in competition with us while they were still on the payroll. The world is full of dodgy people.

By the early part of 2005, we had nine staff and what became very clear was that this business was way too big for our upstairs spare bedroom! We were heading towards a six-figure monthly income but the working environment was cosy to say the least. We had to get out of that bedroom and into a proper office.

This was another lesson learnt because what I thought I would do is buy a big log cabin and put it in my garden. At the time, it seemed a sensible thing to do. I came very close to signing a contract. The guy who was going to sell me the log cabin was a little too pushy, and I refused to sign the contract before going on holiday. That was a smart decision.

There is a common theme throughout my business career, and that is that my holidays are very important to me. They help me reflect. Every time I go away with my family, that little detachment from the business allows me to see things very differently. On most holidays, I make key decisions or change how I see things, and this was certainly one of those instances.

On holiday I realised that if I bought the log cabin that would just about cover the nine people we had, it would give us no scope to expand and grow further. I discovered that I had no desire to run a business from a log cabin that was capped at that level. My ambitions were much bigger than that, so I needed to stay up in the helicopter and think big.

So, I didn't buy the log cabin. I came back from that holiday and went straight to the local estate agent to find the right office premises nearby so I could get a proper office where we would have room to cope with further expansion and that would give us real presence because we were now absolutely, definitely a proper business with a really great future.

Not only was My Mag storming ahead to huge success, but we'd also conceived the next big project that I firmly believed could be even bigger: 'thebestof'.

In February 2005, N5 moved into its first proper office at Olton Bridge, Solihull. It's just over a mile from our home – so not exactly an onerous commute! I bought the building, which was just over 2,000 square feet, we decorated, recarpeted and kitted it out in bright colours and with all the latest technology. All nine staff each had their own workstation. We had loads of space. I predicted that this space would cope with our expansion for at least five years.

But in the end, it didn't cope with our expansion for one year – let alone five …

CHAPTER 5
THEBESTOF LAUNCH

In 2004, we had this huge phenomenon of success with My Mag and the magazines. Sue's magazine had been running for a couple of years at this point. By the end of the year we'd set up several hundred My Maggers – all in the UK.

I'd taken the decision in the summer of 2004 to drop all my consultant clients and close down that part of the business because I had to really see if there was a proper long-term business with My Mag – and I'd never know for certain if I was doing it part time alongside the very demanding consultancy stuff.

The more I got involved with the magazine business, the better I understood the opportunities. It seemed to me that while the magazines were great and were working very well with a lot of success for both us and for the people operating them, at that point the world was starting to move online. The Internet was becoming much more widely used. It had largely been the preserve of businesses to that point, but it was now getting into homes. Broadband was starting to pop up in the UK, and I started wondering if there was a way to take the best elements of the magazines and put them into some kind of online venture.

I knew I had to do something because there were two big problems with the My Mag business. Firstly, we were selling a 'business-in-a-box'. People bought the box and the rights to the postcode area. But that meant we could only sell each postcode area once, and therefore there was a limit to the number of My Mag Packs we could ultimately sell. Our business was definitely finite in that respect.

Secondly, there was no ongoing residual income from My Mag. Once someone had bought the My Mag Pack, they were under no obligation to spend any more money with us. Although, we'd set up a My Mag club to provide support, content, training and to help people with their publications, what we were finding was that they were staying in the club for only about six or seven months. At that point, one of two things happened. In a few cases, they decided the magazine wasn't for them, and they stopped publishing so they had no further use for the club. Or, what happened in most cases, was that people were starting to flourish and thrive with their magazine and, in truth, once you'd been running it for six or seven months, they had no real need for the support they got from the club.

This combination of factors – running out of areas to sell and no ongoing 'back-end' income – meant that we had real challenges coming around the corner at us. The business model either had to have an injection of something else into it or it was going to run out of steam at some point in the next two years.

So started our online journey.

The Internet Is Coming

How could we take all the good things about the magazines and somehow turn them into some kind of online product or service that would be helpful to local people – and to local businesses – and could we make a business out of it?

Sue and I took a short holiday during October half term in 2004. We were walking on a beach in Devon in very windy conditions. We were mapping out how this website might work. Sue came up with a name for it – she's pretty much named all of our businesses. We'd decided that our website would only feature really good businesses and she wanted to call it thebestof. This way, we could have a thebestof in each town.

And so, thebestof was conceived on Woolacombe beach. At that point, the only online business directories in the UK were those run by Yell and Thomson. Both were big household names whose businesses had been built on the back of the printed books that were delivered to houses.

If we were going to launch thebestof, then we were going to be the first independent online directory in the UK, so we were breaking new ground. I came back from that short holiday fired up to get it moving – quickly. I mapped out what I thought we wanted the business to do, and how it would work, and I knew that I needed someone technical to make this happen. I needed a web developer.

Be Careful from whom You Take Advice

I approached John Harper, (he was the guy who'd offered to save me a ton of cash on pay-per-click.) Well, I got to know John quite well. We'd met at some networking events, and he was a very nice chap who worked from home. He had a very bright, switched-on son called Stuart. Stuart was at university studying IT and he was red hot on cutting-edge web development. I thought they'd make a perfect team to build thebestof. (I didn't need their marketing advice – just their technical skills and know-how!)

Botty's Rule No. 10
Exploit the web fully – 'cos most people aren't!

The Internet is here to stay, baby, and super-successful business owners all embrace the web and use it to help them grow their profits, BUT 90% of local businesses are doing nowhere near enough to exploit the potential of the web.

It's been over six years since we launched thebestof and the role that the Internet plays in business has changed immeasurably since then. thebestof is a business with a website, not a website business, but I'm amazed at how few local businesses have really embraced the web and use it to help them develop and grow. At the end of the day, it's just another type of media, but it is a very power-ful one and one that is becoming woven into the very fabric of our society.

Merely having a website doesn't get close to what I mean here. For instance, if you haven't learnt about and experimented with Google AdWords (or pay-per-click, or sponsored links – they're all the same thing), then you are bonkers. I'm serious. For many businesses, there are large numbers of people looking online, in your area, for what you do. What pay-per-click does is give you the oppor-tunity to be found by them quickly and easily. If you haven't learnt how to do that and tested and trialled it, then you have probably made a very big mistake and missed out on thousands of pounds of revenue.

An even bigger omission by many businesses is a fail-ure to be registered on Google Places.

When someone undertakes a 'local search', Google will normally throw back a map at the top of the search results with red pins in it. There are never more than seven pins and each pin relates to a local business that ostensibly provides the service that you have just searched for.

Registering your business with Google Places is free and it takes less than 10 minutes to do, yet it can get your business on the front page of Google every day. Your business can – and will – feature as one of those pins.

In my experience, over 80% of businesses that I talk to have not done this. Completely bonkers.

The key here is that just having a website is nowhere near enough. You have to utilise the Internet to drive leads and enquiries, to build your database and to make sales for your business. If you're not, then, in all likelihood, it offers you the single biggest potential for growth over the next six to nine months.

You can get free access to online training on Google AdWords and instructions on how to get your business registered on Google Places, as well as a two-month free trial of my Entrepreneurs' Circle by visiting **www.nigel botterill.com/bookoffer**.

I spoke with John and briefed him on what I wanted to do. I asked if he'd be interested in building thebestof website for me. With hindsight, approaching John and Stuart was a silly thing to do. Going to a one-man band who was used to building three- to four-page websites for local businesses and asking him to build something as complex as thebestof was extremely naive on my part. It wasn't about his ability – just the size of the task.

In my defence, at that time we didn't know how big it was going to get. I knew John was a good web designer, and at that point what I didn't want to do was shell out thousands of pounds. I was keen to get my ideas developed without committing huge amounts of cash and capital to doing it.

What I suggested to John was that he should do the work and I'd cover his expenses. I'd only pay him a couple of thousand pounds up front, but essentially he would earn his money by taking a share of each franchise sale that I made. I shared with him my plans to grow thebestof quickly, and how initially I would be taking the concept to our My Maggers and offer them the chance to take on this new venture.

I offered to pay him £500 from every franchise sale. This meant that he had the potential to earn a lot of money when we sold a lot of franchises. The website would be mine. It was purely a commission arrangement. He had no share in the business, but he would be paid for every franchise we sold. I'd already identified at that point that there was the potential to sell 400–500 franchises in the UK. He was looking at a contract that potentially was worth £200,000–£300,000 to him over a two- or three-year period. That would be a life-changing sum for him.

Initially, John got very excited about this, so I got the agreement drafted for him, and he started to do some work on the project. He then called me one day and asked to meet. He told me that he'd talked to a solicitor whom he'd asked to go over the agreement I'd put together for him.

The solicitor had explained all the reasons why he shouldn't sign. I'd shared my plan for thebestof with John and that included all the costs that I'd incur setting up the franchise and marketing it. I'd have to employ staff to market and sell hundreds of franchises, and it was going to cost a lot of money to do this. He'd passed all this information on to his solicitor.

She had told him that she thought it was a 'crazy venture' … and that she thought that the cost and revenue projections I'd put together were 'clearly unrealistic'. Her advice to John would be for him not to get involved in any such scheme. As I recall, she actually called it a scheme.

Long story short, John wasn't prepared to sign the agreement. He felt that, following his solicitor's advice, it wouldn't be the right thing to do. He felt that the numbers I'd put forward to him were not generous enough, and we reached an impasse. I was very cross and frustrated with his solicitor's advice. I knew quite a bit about building businesses and I believed his solicitor probably didn't. I was worried for John as well. At this point I knew, just knew, that thebestof was going to be huge success and he was on the verge of walking away from it. It could be the biggest mistake of his life, and he was making it because of what I believed was poor advice from a solicitor who I felt was singularly ill equipped to advise on the topic at all.

She was steering John Harper down a course that was going to end up in disappointment for him. I was very keen to pay him a couple hundred thousand pounds over the next two or three years as we sold these franchises, and I was very confident we'd make those sales. In exchange, I needed to have ownership and copyright of the web code.

He insisted it was a scheme and the forecasts were crazy. I was adamant that it wasn't. I gave him a final four-day deadline to sign the agreement. He didn't sign, so I went off to find someone else to build the website.

That decision ended up costing John over £300,000. It would have completely changed his life. John and I haven't really spoken since he walked away from that 'deal of a life-time' almost six years ago. I don't think we've fallen out – it's just that our paths haven't crossed. John's a lovely guy. Salt of the earth, do-anything-for-anyone type of bloke and I feel very sad that he missed out on being part of the amazing thebestof story. Still, we all have to take responsibility for our decisions, and the decision was his. He made it because of advice from a solicitor who might well be a highly skilled lawyer, but did not seem to be a businesswoman: a different skill altogether.

One Man Misses ... Another Man Scores

It was now getting toward the end of 2004, and I needed a developer quickly because I had big plans, but the website was going to be key to all of this. I asked friends and colleagues that I knew and a good friend of mine, Jason Dalby, a very successful commercial property developer, said he knew a bright guy that had done some work for his business.

He introduced me to a chap named Dave Carruthers. I spoke with Dave on the phone and met him in a little restaurant called Matricardi's in Henley in Arden, Warwickshire. I later found out we met there because Dave had no offices, no premises at all, and neither did I, at that point. We were both still working from home.

I sat down with him and over a cappuccino mapped out what I was planning to do. Dave got very excited. It was clear that he was a very enthusiastic guy. He was only 22 when I met him, and I asked him if he could build this. 'Yes, of course. No problem,' he said.

What I found out subsequently was that Dave had no idea how on earth he was going to build it. He didn't have the skills needed to build this type of website. But he was very excited about the prospect, and he wasn't going to let the small matter of inadequate programming skills get in the way.

Dave has a very can-do attitude. It's one of his biggest strengths and so he started building thebestof. I later found out that he worked 24/7 for quite a lot of weeks to build this website. I'd offered him exactly the same agreement that I'd offered John Harper. Dave grabbed it with both hands. He never saw a lawyer. He signed the agreement and over the next three years he earned over £400,000 from it.

Secret Meetings

I knew that it's much easier to sell stuff to existing customers than it is to new people. The fact is that existing customers know you, they trust you (assuming you've done a good job in the past) and they're prepared to listen to you much more easily than Joe Public who has never heard of you before. With this in mind, in the spring of 2005, I wrote a letter to all the My Maggers. We had over 400 of them at that point. I told them that I had something really exciting to share with them, and I invited them to a 'Secret Meeting' to find out more. We really bigged up the 'Shh, it's a secret, don't tell anybody …' There were six Secret Meetings, held on consecutive days in Leeds, Manchester, Cambridge,

Birmingham, Reading and London, and they took place in the early evening.

What we would do is set off after lunch for each venue. I got a chauffeur for a big Mercedes van and four of my team and I, including Dave Carruthers, would travel to another place each day.

I'd set the dates of these Secret Meetings quite a few weeks in advance, and in doing that, what I'd done, consciously, is create the deadline, by which time we had to have thebestof ready to go. (Remember Botty's Rule No. 5!)

There was a lot to sort out. It wasn't just about getting the website done but also the franchise agreement, the training material, the manuals for the franchise; all the ancillary market-ing materials to actually build the business had to be completed. We built it all in less than four months. Looking back, that drive to do it quickly helped us hugely. It focused everyone on delivery, and it ensured that we got the product out there soon enough to capitalise on a huge opportunity.

I led the Secret Meetings and really sold the vision by explaining why the magazines had been so successful and the fact that the world was moving online. I articulated in a reasonably convincing manner why thebestof represented the future for these magazine publishers. It offered them significant revenue opportunities and the chance to broaden and grow their business, and play an even more valuable part in their local communities.

The initial thebestof proposition was essentially an online web directory – the first independent online web directory in the UK. We were planning to have fairly high dependency on Google presence in the beginning and were going to support that with an extensive Google AdWords pay-per-click campaign. In short, our initial proposition was that, for £10 per month, we'd get local businesses featured high up on Google, via thebestof website.

Businesses would pay just £10 per month to be featured on thebestof, and I felt this was a real masterstroke at the time, because it was such a ridiculously small sum of money for businesses to pay. I just knew that they would do it in conjunction with all their other marketing. Ten pounds a month would not be something anyone would worry about, therefore we were not competing with the existing and established advertising media. People would do this as well as, not instead of.

In addition to that, the website would be a great ad for the magazine businesses that all these My Maggers were running.

I've got to tell you, if you want to get traction and build momentum in a business, running a launch like we did with thebestof (with the six Secret Meetings in six days) is unquestionably the way to get it moving. Building the hype and anticipation, which we did, plays a big part in success. Apple, of course, has mastered it in modern times with the launch of the upgrades of the iPhone and iPad but the principles they adopt and use are exactly the same as we were deploying five years earlier, albeit in a somewhat more modest way!

I've repeated it subsequently with other product launches, but thebestof was the first time we'd done it. As a result, we had 47 franchisees contracted and on board before we launched thebestof, which still, to this day, is completely unprecedented in UK franchising.

Our Secret Meeting launch plan meant that I was able to present thebestof to over 350 very interested people in six days. The concept of one (i.e., me) selling to many is a very effective way to generate business and generate sales – when you've got a group of people who are interested.

I knew from some of our mistakes with My Mag that it was key that we did everything right with thebestof. We'd learnt a lot of lessons. thebestof was set up as a proper franchise. We had a franchise agreement that I spent many thousands of pounds getting drafted and written up properly by specialist franchise lawyers. (Our franchise agreement was written by Peter Manford, a partner at Martineau Johnson in Birmingham.) Peter has looked after us very well over the years. Looking back, one of the smartest things I ever did was spending the £12,000 it cost me to get thebestof franchise agreement written and drafted by specialist franchise lawyers. There is no substitute for having the right legal documentation – there's no way you should ever cut corners on that – and that money has paid for itself many times over in subsequent years.

Pantomimes and the BFA

In working towards doing everything right, I thought we'd better join the British Franchise Association. I contacted them in May before we launched the franchise to apply to join. They sent the application forms, I filled them in and sent them back. They said I couldn't apply until the franchise was actually launched, and we hadn't launched yet.

We took the forms and submitted them again on 2 July 2005 – the day after we went live.

On the forms it asked for date of launch – 1 July 2005 – and number of franchisees – 47. The forms were posted, and I got a phone call a week or so later from a woman from the BFA. She said there seemed to be some mistakes in the application. I apologised and asked what the problem was.

She said, 'It says here that you launched on the first of July.'

'Yes, that's right.' I said.

'But you say you have 47 franchisees, and that can't be right ...'

'It is right' I explained.

'That's impossible,' she replied.

I told the woman from the BFA what we'd done. She just didn't get it – or believe it. The lady I spoke to told me it simply wasn't possible to have 47 franchisees in the same week as you launched a franchise business.

I said, 'Well, we do.'

She said, 'You can't have.'

It was like a pantomime.

I directed her to the website where she could see all my franchisees. I wanted the BFA to see that this was a bona fide business and to see for herself the way the business was structured and set up.

This was such an unusual situation for the BFA, they just had no idea how to deal with it. They'd never seen anything like it before, and they didn't know what to do. It would normally take several years to get to 47 franchisees – in fact, most franchises never even get to that number – so for us to do it in our first week was completely unprecedented. What we'd done went against every established norm that they understood. We had rocked their world.

They wouldn't approve our membership to the BFA, but neither could they reject us because there were no grounds for rejection.

The situation dragged on for almost a year.

After almost 12 months, in May 2006, they invited me to join and I declined. I told them that I really needed them a year ago, when we launched, but by the time they accepted me, we had over 200 franchisees and I didn't need

Botty's Rule No. 11
Most people in your industry or sector are wrong ... about everything.

This is something that I came to realise from the launch and development of thebestof. You see, in any group of people, you'll be able to break it down into roughly these percentages – 5%, 15%, 60% and 20%.

It doesn't matter whether the group is franchisees in thebestof or hairdressers across the UK, it will break down, broadly, into those percentages. Here's what those percentages represent in business terms: 5% are very successful, 15% are getting there, 60% are getting by and 20%, at any one time, are struggling.

Stop to think about the implications of that analysis for a moment. You'll soon come to the inescapable conclusion that most people in your industry or sector are wrong – about everything. Because most people are in the 60% and the 20%.

If you were to look at that group as franchisors in the UK, then, by any definition, we are in the top 5%. Over the last six years, we have rewritten the rules of franchising in the UK. We didn't do this deliberately; it's just that we set up thebestof without realising that what we had put into place was almost the polar opposite of established practices among franchisors.

The fact that we did everything very differently and are in the top 5% is not a coincidence. And so it is in every sector. So work out who the 5% are in your sector or industry and then make it your business to find out

what it is that they are doing differently to everybody else because only lazy, unambitious, unimaginative business owners follow the crowd … don't they?

You cannot ignore this. If you follow the crowd and do what everybody else does, then you'll get the results that everybody else gets and those results will be mediocre and average. You will not become super-successful by doing what everybody else does. Break the mould.

their endorsement or approval. Any help they could give me in terms of credibility and stature was long gone. So, we never joined the BFA because they just didn't get our business model.

There's an interesting lesson here, I think. If you want to be super-successful in your sector, then what you have to do is be different from everyone else at what you do. In my experience, the more different you are, the better. There are hundreds of franchise companies in the UK, and none of them did things like we did back in 2005. (Quite a few do now, by the way!) We have rewritten the rules of franchising over the last five years since we launched thebestof. We're in the top 1% of franchisors, by pretty much any measure, and it's because so many of the things we do are completely different to how the rest of the franchise market does them. I believe those two things are very connected and that's why, if you want to achieve super-success, doing things differently to how the rest of your market does it, is really key.

Induction

On the back of the momentum created by the Secret Meetings, we started to bring a whole host of franchisees on board, and we got some really brilliant people in that first wave of franchisees during the summer of 2005. One such couple were Kevin and Pamela Bourne, who came to our first-ever induction course for thebestof.

It was a one-day course where we taught new franchisees everything about how this business worked – from how to position it, how to market it, how to get customers, etc. Kevin and Pamela came to see me at the end of that induction course. They'd just flown back into the country the night before from their home in France. They explained that as they only landed yesterday and had to set up their new home in England, they were not going to be the fastest out of the blocks. But Kevin made a promise to me at that meeting that he would become our most successful franchisee within six months. He did pretty well. He got up there because he had the focus, the energy and the drive to make it happen. He was running thebestof in Redhill and Reigate and subsequently, he also bought thebestof in Bromley, one of the big London boroughs, and did a great job with that, too.

Another early franchisee who went on to have great success was Nick Taimitarha, who joined us the second half of 2005 to run thebestof Richmond. Nick has built a really fantastic business in Richmond, and he personifies everything that is great about the business. He is well regarded by local business owners and has a fab reputation. He's also very innovative and has been among the key players in our network that have helped us to develop the proposition and take it from being just an online directory and turned it into something much more substantial, useful and helpful for local businesses.

Nick's networking meetings and how he plugs business owners together is legendary within our network – and also within Richmond and beyond. He plays a huge part in generating commerce and making business happen in the borough, and it's been a real pleasure and a privilege to work with him over the last five years.

Strange Franchisees

Not everybody has been a roaring success. We had one or two challenges and issues as well. We had one guy who bought thebestof franchise in his local area. He appeared to be the ideal franchisee. He was great at growing the business quicker than anyone else in the network at that time. Any incentive or competition we ran, he either won or came in second or third. He was very outspoken about the work ethic that was required to build a successful thebestof business, and we used him quite a bit in the early years of the business as something of a figurehead of an ideal franchisee.

It was only much later that we realised that a lot of what he'd done was built on sand. Not everything was as it seemed in his business. He'd duplicated a lot of things to make his figures look bigger and better. This was an interesting lesson. Not everybody shares the same values and ethics in business. Some people do have different drivers and, when you're building a large network and they are trading under your brand, you have to be careful.

Another strange story also occurred in London. We had one guy pay over £30,000 for one of our largest franchise areas, and he did absolutely nothing with it. Ever. He never came to the induction course. He never signed up a business. He never did anything with his website or anything else, for that matter. We tried to contact him, to no avail. It was like he just disappeared. After only a few weeks we had no choice but to terminate his franchise. It was very bizarre. He paid us a big chunk of money and just walked away. As we say in Yorkshire, 'There's nowt so queer as folk!'

What I learnt as we started to work closely with franchisees is that not everyone is as driven and as focused as I am, or as I'd like them to be. Things that were obvious to me were not always obvious to other people. Some people are very lazy; others don't think as much as they ought to. It is a real challenge managing and motivating a large network of franchisees because, by definition, it's very eclectic.

You have this split. It's the same split I talked of in Botty's Rule No. 11 where there's a small percentage of people who are right at the top who do very well and become very wealthy and are super-successful.

Then there's a really big chunk – typically 60% or so of people – who are in the middle. These people do okay; they get by. They're not super-successful, but neither are they destined for failure, and that's where the biggest chunk of people sit. They kind of just plod along.

In any population of people, you have a smaller group at the bottom, maybe as much as 20%, who are struggling. I think these numbers apply whether it's children in a class at school, businesses in a certain town or in this case, franchisees of thebestof. We continually have our top 20% or, our bottom 20% and a big chunk of people somewhere in the middle. It has been a real challenge to switch on and motivate as many people as we can and try to move them into that top group. It's not easy.

One of the challenges we have in this regard is that when we started to sell thebestof, if you came along to see us and had a cheque for the right amount and wanted to buy a franchise, I would sell you one. I wasn't as discerning in the beginning as I ought to have been about whom we sold franchises to. We're much tighter now and have been for several years, but in the beginning we pretty much let anyone in.

That means that, with hindsight, we recruited a bunch of franchisees who, frankly, it would've been better if they'd not joined us. A few are still with us but most have gone now. However, it certainly isn't the case any more. We're really rigorous in our selection criteria, almost to the point where I worry sometimes that we might be overcautious.

For instance, we've got a really great franchisee in Gloucester called Clive Hannis. Clive joined us in 2006, but I wonder whether, if Clive was to apply now, he would get in. Clive had a background in manufacturing. He had little of the obvious skills that you would expect should be necessary to succeed in this business. He'd never really used a computer before. He'd not sold anything of great significance. And yet he became one of our more successful franchisees, despite on paper not having what you would assume would be the right level of skills needed to be successful.

He applied himself with great energy and vigour and built a very successful business for himself and his wife Carole, which was just fantastic. He was in many ways the exception that proved the rule in those early days and I was very pleased for Clive and Carole when they won our Franchisee of the Year Award in 2007.

Copycats

While thebestof was rocketing away, My Mag was still contributing hugely to the business. However, in early 2006, we had a really painful episode with My Mag. A lady had bought My Mag a year or so earlier. She'd been very successful with it, and decided that she'd repay that success we'd helped her to have by copying our My Mag model. And she had launched herself in direct competition to us.

We'd known this lady and had spent a bit of time with her. It was especially hard for Sue and I to handle when it first happened; we took it very personally. It felt like we'd been mugged or burgled. It was emotionally very distressing, and we just couldn't understand how someone could do something like this. I got lawyers involved and was all set to pursue her through the courts for the damage that she was causing us.

We went to great lengths to get copies of all her material. I employed barristers and solicitors. It all came to a head when one day I had to go to London. I met my solicitor at Birmingham International Railway Station. We travelled down to Euston first-class. Then we got a taxi across to Royal Mint Court, where we met in chambers with a barrister who specialised in this type of action.

We spent two or three hours with this barrister, then got on the train back home again. Only when I got back that evening did I realise that I'd just incurred costs that day of something like £4,000 on solicitor's fees, barrister's fees and travel costs. I got on the phone with my colleague and friend, Bill Glazer. It was clearly causing me a lot of angst and anxiety, and Bill asked me why I was pursuing this.

I got quite emotional and explained that we felt we'd been exploited and ripped off. In a very calm manner he let me know why pursuing this legal action was really the wrong thing to do. It was going to consume my energy and time, as it had done that previous day. It would cost a lot of money. The real cost of pursuing this rather than focusing on developing and growing my business was something that Bill talked to me about and advised against. He said, 'Nige, you've built something here that's hugely successful. People are bound to want to copy and replicate it. I'm only surprised it's taken this long …' His advice was very clear: let it go. Walk away from it.

After a good night's sleep, I realised what wise words those had been, and I followed Bill's advice. I dropped all legal action and walked away from it.

Subsequently, we've had many copycats with thebestof. We spawned an industry in its own right, having been the first independent online directory.

Loads of people tried to copy us. Most of them came and went very quickly. One was even set up by an ex-employee who ripped us off, but again, I learnt from that initial My Mag case, that the right thing to do is focus on your own game. You can't copyright an idea, but what you can do is implement it really well and drive it forward, so that's what we spent our time focusing on. It's an attitude and approach that has served us really well.

All in all, thebestof got off to a real flying start and great progress was made in those first 12 months. We built a large franchise network very quickly. That network was growing fast, we had thousands of businesses on board and, together with our franchisees, we were building something that had all the potential to become very big, very quickly.

CHAPTER 6
THEBESTOF – PART II

We were able to build on the momentum of having the 47 franchises on day one and recruited over 200 franchisees to thebestof before the end of our first 12 months.

This was completely unprecedented, and we became the fastest growing UK franchise ever. We now have over 400 franchises. Very few UK franchises have ever gone beyond 400, and those that have, have done it over a much longer period of time.

There were several things that were key to our success in driving this rapid growth. The first was my unrelenting focus on the marketing of the business. I always knew that our success would depend on our ability to market our business effectively, so that's what I spent most of my time and energy doing. I built a good team of people around me and I delegated as much as I could – with the exception of the marketing, which I knew had to be my domain.

Every morning I'd arrive at the office, shut my office door and spend 90 minutes working, uninterrupted, on the marketing.

We also kept pushing the price up. That's another lesson I had learnt with My Mag in the previous couple of years. Those franchisees that came to the Secret Meetings were able to buy into thebestof for less than £4,000. Two years later, if

Botty's Rule No. 12
Getting and keeping customers – your first job every day.

The first thing that super-successful business owners do every morning is the most important, most critical thing for the success of their business … it's marketing.

I learnt this rule from a very wise man called Martin Howey. Not long after I'd set up N5, I was talking with Martin, and he asked me what was the most important thing that I had to achieve if my business was going to be successful. Its an awkward question, but I finally settled on, 'Getting new customers and keeping the ones I've got.'

Martin agreed: as long as I was getting a regular flow of new customers and keeping the ones that I already had, then everything else in my business could and would be taken care of – but without that regular flow of customers, I didn't have a business at all. He went on to explain to me how getting and keeping customers is all about marketing.

He then asked what I'd done first thing that morning. In common with many people, I suspect, my answer was that I'd checked my email, checked the voice mails, briefed the staff, made a couple of phone calls and started doing some work.

'That's interesting,' he said, 'but when are you going to do the marketing today?'

'I hadn't planned on doing any marketing today,' I replied.

'But you said that marketing is the most important thing for the success of your business, so why would you not only not do it first thing in the morning but not plan to do any at all today?' Martin asked me, surprised.

It was a very salutary lesson and one that I implemented immediately. From that day on, I've established a regular routine. My working day typically begins around 7.30 a.m. When I arrive, I shut my door and hang up a little sign that says, **'Do not disturb unless building is on fire.'** The phone is off the hook, my email is turned off and I spend at least 90 minutes doing marketing for my business.

This is probably the most productive habit I have ever developed. It has been worth literally millions of pounds to me. You see, when I emerge from my office to confront the rigours of the day, it doesn't really matter what happens because I've already done the marketing. This has ensured that our business has kept on the front foot, that we've always had very strong growth curves.

Like I said, it's a habit, and it's one that many other super-successful business owners have, as well. I know, because they've told me. I commend it to you, especially if marketing is not what you're good at. If you're like most business owners, then the marketing is difficult, it's a chore, it's out of your comfort zone. If that's you, then you're at even greater risk of not getting the marketing done unless you get into the habit of making it the first thing you do every morning!

you wanted to buy the rights to a large town in the UK, you were paying £30,000–£35,000.

These regular price increases, allied of course to genuine scarcity because we could only have one franchisee in each town, and some fabulous success stories made thebestof more and more desirable. It also encouraged people to take action, because if they committed and bought the franchise, they'd lock in at the lower price before the increase happened.

With all the copycats that came out of the woodwork, we steadfastly refused to compete on price. We were always the most expensive franchise of our type – always – and I was determined that we always would be. We shouted a lot about being 'the original and the best', and the price supported that. We were also in it for the long term and our commitment to developing the business and supporting franchisees demonstrated that to any serious candidates.

'I'm a Franchisee, Ask Me'

One of our biggest sources of new franchisees were the franchise exhibitions that are held in the UK. There are four exhibitions each year: London, Manchester, Birmingham (the biggest one of the year at the NEC) and Scotland.

We did the exhibitions very differently from anybody else, and it's no coincidence that we have consistently been more successful than any other franchise at recruiting more new franchisees at each exhibition we go to.

We turned up at our first exhibition with three members of my team and four franchisees. We were all wearing our 'uniform' of smart jeans with some nicely branded polo or rugby shirts, all branded up in thebestof colours and on the back of the franchisees shirts it said, in big letters, 'I'm a Franchisee, Ask Me.'

We just cleaned up at our early exhibitions. I mean, we properly crushed it. Our stand was rammed from the minute the exhibition opened until half an hour after it closed. On one occasion we sold 23 franchisees on the back of a single exhibition – which is unheard of in the industry, where most franchisors are happy if they make one sale.

One of the reasons for our success was because all the other exhibitors were dressed in suits with ties and clipboards. If people are coming to an exhibition because they're considering buying into a franchise, they don't want to talk to men in suits. They want to talk to normal people, people like them. By dressing in jeans and our polo shirts, we made ourselves 'normal' and approachable, but at the time it was radical stuff in the franchise industry. (Although I'm pleased to say that plenty of switched-on franchisors have since seen the light!)

More than anything, though, the reason for our success at exhibitions was our franchisees. People just wanted to talk to them, and we were the first people to put franchisees on our stands. Now, over the last four or five years, a lot of other franchisors have worked out why we always had such a large crowd at our exhibition stand, and why we were signing up so many new franchisees as a result, so they copied our approach and started bringing their franchisees along.

You see, more than anything else, prospective franchisees want to talk to existing franchisees, and by having them there and available, we were able to meet that need. And in the early days, we really played on this point: 'You have to ask yourself why no one else here today has franchisees on their stand ...'

The bottom line is that we did things differently, and that was a real key element in our growth. Without meaning to, we have rewritten many of the rules of franchising in the UK over the last five years. Our progressive techniques have now become the norm, adopted and copied by many.

Always Changing, Always Innovating

In 2006, we began running Discovery Days, and we still run them very successfully today. They're very effective for us. We direct a lot of our marketing to pulling people into our head office once a month for a three- to four-hour session.

We've got some really well-kitted-out training rooms at our Solihull HQ where we train all our franchisees. (They're in use two to three days every week). At our Discovery Days we bring prospective franchisees into those training rooms where they can meet existing franchisees, myself and the management team. We allow them to really 'kick the tyres' of the whole business and get all their questions answered. They get a whole picture. This technique of presenting 'one-to-many' works very well and it helps to shorten the cycle and get them to a position more quickly as to whether this is something they want to do or not. As I mentioned earlier, we are quite fussy about who we accept as franchisees now, and by involving my whole management team, plus some existing franchisees, in these Discovery Days, we get a very good feel as to the suitability of the people who come along to run a successful thebestof franchise.

These Discovery Days were another innovation in the franchise industry, which has been copied by many.

As well as marketing the franchise effectively, we were also developing the business that our franchisees were offering. We introduced things like 'Talking Testimonials', which already now, just five years later, seem quite archaic. When people went to the page on which a particular florist was featured, they would hear that florist talking to them. It was quite novel, and in 2006 really quite exciting stuff. I know now with the advent of YouTube and everything else, that looks almost passé, but it was cutting-edge in its time. Honestly!

We also gave our franchisees access to really smart, leading-edge marketing tools. I used to go to marketing conferences in the States and bring back stuff to the UK that was unheard of and unseen over here. We were the first to do a lot of things in the UK from a marketing perspective because our marketing focus was really key.

The First Million ...

There was one very memorable day on 16 September 2006. Brenda Brown, my bookkeeper, came to see me, with a print-out of our bank statement for that day. She passed it to me silently with a smile on her face. For the first time, our bank account had over £1 million pounds in it.

Let me tell you, it was a tremendous feeling, and Sue and I did crack a small bottle of bubbly that night.

The next day I rang Noel Farrelly (remember him?) and told him I'd found him another client!

Should You Employ Friends?

Growing the business is one thing, but what you have to do in a franchise network is support that growth. That meant me bringing on people to run what we call our Franchisee Development Team.

I was a little unsure as to how I was going to pull this together. I knew I needed to get good people in, but I was very unsure about where to go. I was reluctant to go to established franchisors and try to hire staff that had experience in the industry because I knew by now that so much of what we were doing was different to industry norms in the UK. Our way seemed to be working pretty well, and I didn't want to risk jeopardising that by bringing someone in who would have a lot of baggage.

This wasn't a role I could bring young kids into, either. The right person needed to have some life experience to be able to support and command the respect of my franchisees.

We had a whole list of things that our franchisees needed help with. It wasn't just technical help and training; it was also sales and marketing training. We had to motivate these people as well. We had to inspire them. We had to act as counsellors when things went wrong in their lives as well as in their businesses. When you've got a large network, someone needs help with all of these situations pretty much every week.

I was mulling over what I should do. One night I'd come home early from work because Sue had booked some tickets for us to go and see the Osmonds in concert in Birmingham. We like to go to concerts. Sue and I are lucky to live close to both the NEC and the NIA, so we get to go see a lot of world-famous acts.

I have to say that going to see the Osmonds was not something I was particularly excited about, but Sue had grown up idolising Donny Osmond and his brothers. They were touring again, and she really wanted to go, so I was happy to get some tickets. We took a couple of friends along, Lorna and Stuart Bevins. Stu was a former first-class cricketer, who'd played for Worcestershire, as a wicket keeper. His cricket career had finished a few years earlier, and he was now working in his father's print and stationery business.

While the ladies got very excited about the Osmonds over dinner, Stuart and I got talking about business. I explained my challenges with thebestof, and the franchise network. He then started to share with me some of his frustrations at working with his dad and how he was finding it really quite difficult. He felt he ought to think about doing something different.

I was very wary about recruiting a friend, having had quite an unpleasant experience previously doing just that, but when we came home that night, as we were getting ready for bed, I asked Sue if she thought Stuart would make a good franchisee development manager, as he seemed to tick a lot of the boxes. Sue was wary. We just didn't want to employ friends again after what had happened last time. While she agreed that his personality and sports background were ideal, she felt I should let it drop. Lorna and Stuart were such good friends that she didn't want anything to jeopardise the friendship. Employing friends, we decided as we went to sleep, was a bad thing.

Next morning, I got a call from Stu. Turned out he'd kept Lorna up most of the night talking through what a really good job he could do for us and why it would be a great move for him. He asked if we could meet up and talk about it because he'd really like to come and work for me.

I invited him around to our house that evening and the three of us had a very open and frank conversation. Long story short, Stuart joined the business to head up my franchisee development team. He's still with me today, over four years later, and he's a really critical and key member of my management team. He's undertaken several different roles in the business and is someone I can rely on completely. He's so committed, and he's played a big part in driving our business forward and delivering such a lot of success over the last four years. I'm really glad he joined us, and I'm grateful for all he has done to build the business. On this occasion, employing a friend has worked out really well.

The Makings of a Good Team …

Not long after Stu came on board, I was driving home one evening when I took a phone call. It was a number I didn't recognise and a very bright, sparkly lady introduced herself to me as Michelle Downey. She explained that she was the best franchisee development manager in the country.

She went on to tell me that she'd heard and seen what we were doing with thebestof and wanted to come work with us because she felt she could make a real difference to our business. She was so confident and assured, and so engaging in her conversation, that I thought the least I could do would be to agree to meet her.

I invited her to come for an interview the following week and I was completely taken with her whole personality and her drive, as well as her track record and experience. It was easy to see what a great asset she would be to the business and so I offered her a job in the franchisee development team, working with Stu. Her enthusiasm and passion shines just as brightly today as it did when she first joined us, and Michelle now heads up our franchisee development team. She is loved and respected by all our franchisees and she's another key member of the gang.

At this point, Dave Carruthers was still with me, taking his very chunky commission cheques each month as we sold more and more franchises. He was helping to develop the business, but he was also getting itchy feet and wanting to do his own thing.

I had the makings of a good team here. We had the right attitude across the workforce. The vibe was great. It's impossible to build any kind of sizeable, successful business without having a good bunch of people around you. I was very fortunate with people like Stuart, Dave, Michelle and Mike Giles (who was a key member of my gang for four years before he went solo on the entrepreneurial trail). They were a very strong team and, together, we made a lot of stuff happen.

It was a young team – only Stu was over 30 – and they all shared my enthusiasm and passion. We became very good at execution and implemented things very quickly. As with any team, what you have to do as the business owner is be prepared to let them take on responsibility, and let them do what they're best at. Like many entrepreneurs, this was not something I found particularly easy.

Because I'd done every job in the business, I had very high standards and it was very difficult for people to do things in quite the way I would've done them. I had to work really hard at this. In fact, it's a challenge that I still have to battle with today.

Intermission

Fast-forward a few years. I had a real defining moment in April 2010 when I realised just how far my team had come. We had our National Conference for thebestof and our annual Celebration Ball coming up on 23 April. Three weeks before the event I jetted off to Egypt for a fortnight's holiday with Sue and the children. I would still have a full week once I came back to rehearse and prepare for the conference, but unfortunately, we got stuck in Egypt as the blasted Icelandic volcano erupted when Europe was plunged into flight chaos.

The plan was that I would take the lead role at the conference, as I always did. I would deliver most of the content, but then I got stuck in Egypt. I couldn't get back for the conference and my team had to step up and take on the role of running and presenting it.

As it happened, I got back just in the nick of time, just a few hours before the conference started. It was too late to change anything, so my team ran the whole event, and I was just so immensely proud of what they did. I realised how good they were and how all the concerns that I'd had over the years about letting go and relinquishing responsibility really had been unfounded. I should've moved much quicker, because I had good people. I should've had more confidence to follow through and let them take up the baton and run with it.

We Need More Room …

Okay, back to 2006–07. We did a good job of developing thebestof during its first couple of years. We'd had to expand into a bigger office building just 14 months after buying our first (fortunately the unit next door was 'for sale' so I bought it and still, to this day, we operate out of these two 'next-door' buildings).

The Power of One

Lots of competitors had sprung up. In addition, we also started to see and identify new opportunities for thebestof, often with help from our franchisees, people like Nick Taimitarha in Richmond and Kevin Bourne, whom I mentioned earlier, David Fernando and Andrew Marsh in Wimbledon and Maud Alleyne in Croydon. These were people who were coming up with good ideas as to how we could develop and improve the business – and we listened.

One franchisee in particular, Simon Bullingham in Cheltenham, was a constant source of new ideas and initiatives. We saw there was a really huge opportunity for us to take thebestof into another league altogether.

We already had a big network. We had tens of thousands of businesses on board but we could see that there were a lot of things businesses needed that we were uniquely positioned to deliver.

I took my then management team – Mike Giles, Dave Carruthers, Stuart Bevins and myself – down to my house in Cornwall for three days in May 2007. There, as the sea crashed onto the rocks outside, we mapped out on huge pieces of paper what we thought thebestof should and could look like, taking on board all the input and ideas from franchisees around the country.

What we mapped out on those large sheets of paper was a really powerful proposition, but it was a very different one compared to the online directory model that we had launched with two years earlier. It was a big, big change. The last thing I did before we left Trevone to head back up the M5 was set the deadline for us to make all this happen. I made a couple of calls and scheduled a big national conference for 3 July 2007. I invited all our franchisees, and their staff, and booked the Ricoh Arena in Coventry. Four hundred and fifty franchisees and their staff turned up for what was a huge, themed event. Setting the deadline had been important to ensure we implemented on time!

We called the event The Power of One (Hey, it had worked well for me at Barclays and it was my theme, after all!), and it was a complete relaunch of thebestof. It was designed to take thebestof properly into the twenty-first century and to catapult us so far ahead of our competitors that our business

Botty's Rule No. 13
'I think big. Most people think small. This gives me a distinct advantage.'

I first learnt this rule in October 2004 when I was fortunate enough to be at a dinner in the States at which Donald Trump was speaking. Trump gave a very forgettable after-dinner speech but then the floor was opened up for Q&A. One very loud Texan asked 'The Donald', 'You are an incredibly successful businessperson. To what do you attribute your success?' Trump replied, 'I think big. Most people think small. This gives me a distinct advantage.'

It was like being whacked around the face by a 20-pound haddock. It had such a profound effect on me, and I still tingle today when I think and talk about that evening.

I think we've been pretty good at 'living' by this mantra in my business ever since that day, but never more so than in the summer of 2007 when we completely relaunched thebestof. We laid out some extraordinarily ambitious plans of which I feel sure Donald himself would have been proud!

Truth is, without diligently following this rule, there is no way that we would have had even a small fraction of the success that we've enjoyed over the last seven or eight years. Thinking big has been critical to so much of what we've done. It's so unusual in business to meet big thinkers. Donald Trump is right: most people do think small. If you want to achieve super-success, then thinking big is a critical place to start.

would become virtually unassailable. This was a huge event with an ambitious agenda for the business. We were definitely thinking big.

Everyone was seated cabaret style. There were three stages, all in the round, and it was basically me on stage for the whole day.

I unveiled a completely new business.

We introduced elements of print to thebestof through our Door Drops and Little Blue Books. Our Door Drops are the swankiest leaflets you've ever seen. They feature 15 of our 'best' businesses – each with a great offer to promote – and they are delivered through letterboxes by Royal Mail. They typically go to 20,000 or 30,000 homes in each franchise area and are published either monthly or quarterly, depending on the franchisee.

We introduced certificates where our franchisees recognised their member businesses officially as the best businesses in their town when those businesses got recommended and received testimonials from a certain number of their customers. This simple element had such a big impact with our customers. No one had given them a certificate since they were at school and they loved the recognition. Sure enough, the certificates were displayed prominently in their shops and receptions. This was great branding and awareness building for us.

We introduced reviews and testimonials onto the website to give local people a voice, which was very cutting-edge at that time. No one else had done that – but once again we were hurriedly copied by many.

We introduced monthly awards: each month in each town we would invite local people to vote and tell us about the best restaurant or the best beauty salon or the best accountancy practice or whatever else the category might be that month. We had a different category each month, with the winners decided by public vote.

We introduced 'Mix and match', giving our franchisees a process whereby they are proactively seeking to plug different business members together so that they are able to do business together. 'Mix and match' has become a really important and valuable part of our proposition and our franchisees have generated millions of pounds of business for their customers though it in the first three years.

By introducing all these different offline elements, we were able to increase the price of being a member of thebestof and really position ourselves as a 'club' of the best businesses in each town. It's an exclusive club, where you have to be recommended to join.

We decided to make thebestof more selective – we would only work with the best businesses. Since 2007, you have to have customers saying why you are the best at what you do and other businesses advocating your membership before you can come on board. This very strong positioning differentiates us hugely from our competition.

I employed a really excellent branding agency, a company called The House, who were introduced to me by James Tribe, one of our franchisees in Bath.

James had met the guys at The House, Steve Fuller and Graham Massey, and they were very excited about our project. They played a huge part in developing the new thebestof branding, our new visual identity and, behind that, developing real clarity as to what our brand stood for and what we were all about.

They really helped us to create this essence of thebestof, about finding the best local businesses by listening to local people and then shouting about these great businesses in lots of different ways, hence the online elements and the print as well.

We put a great little movie together called *The Boy who Cried Best*, which articulated in a powerful way what our new concept was all about.

We unveiled all of this stuff and more at the Ricoh that day. It was described by one franchisee as 'shock and awe'.

While I positioned it very openly at the beginning of the day, I knew that a number of our franchisees would either not be willing or wouldn't be capable of making this transformation with us, but I also knew that for our best franchisees, this was our only chance of keeping them and of giving them an opportunity to build very substantial businesses on their patch. They would become complete marketing partners for their customers – providing an incredible array of solutions at amazing value.

We had to develop the business. We had to move ourselves away from the competition, establish our unique positioning and give our franchisees the opportunity to help local businesses in ways that had never been contemplated before and in doing so, build big businesses for themselves and their families.

Having good partnerships, partners that understand your business and properly work with you, is hugely valuable. They're not just suppliers. There's much more to it than that.

It Was like Being on the *Titanic* ...

There was a lot of fallout from the Power of One event. As I'd said on stage that morning, I knew it wouldn't be for everybody, but I hadn't expected the impact to be quite as big as it was. Literally speaking, a third of the franchisees loved the new proposition that we'd launched, a third hated it and a third were so shocked that they didn't know what to think!

One of the phrases I got thrown at me a lot at that time was, 'This isn't what we bought into ... we bought a web directory franchise.' My answer to them was that this was a little bit like being on the *Titanic* after it hit the iceberg and refusing to get into a lifeboat because you bought a ticket for a luxury liner. At some point it was going to sink, and you would die unless you sought refuge in the lifeboat.

I truly believed that our web directory model was finite – that the market was becoming commoditised and that with the plethora of competition emerging it would not be possible to make a long-term business out of just offering online ads. And so it has proved.

Botty's Rule No. 14
There is no status quo.

Everything happens faster nowadays. Nothing stays the same.

The bottom line is that your business is a living, dynamic organism, and it's either growing or it's shrinking. There is no such thing as stable or static, which is why we were right to progress such an ambitious agenda of change with thebestof in the summer of 2007.

New competitors emerge with much higher frequency than ever before. New opportunities arrive even quicker.

We hold three regional meetings yearly with thebestof franchisees. We introduce one or more new elements to thebestof proposition. It's a discipline for us to ensure that we keep growing.

Whatever business you are in, if you want to secure your future and your lifestyle and you aspire to super-success, then you have to ensure that you are growing, markedly. It's the only way to flourish. There really is no status quo.

We had to do something else if we wanted to thrive and survive – in the same way that it was not possible to get to America if you stayed on the *Titanic*.

Our franchise agreement came under quite a bit of scrutiny. A number of franchisees sought to challenge what we were doing under the terms of their franchise agreement, but the minute they took any kind of legal advice, they realised we were rock solid in that respect. The agreement was working well, but there was no point in hiding behind an agreement. I had to have people on board with their hearts and minds, not just their legal contract. Our franchisees had to really buy into this business and be energised by it if they were going to succeed. It was hard.

I think every bit of our thinking and concept that we unveiled in the summer of 2007 was absolutely bang on. So many of our online directory competitors have either fallen by the wayside or else have stagnated and are at a very low level of income and operation, whereas thebestof has flourished and thrived like never before on the back of what was a very bold set of decisions and initiatives that we took back then.

You Can Take a Horse to Water ...

On the back of the Power of One event, we made it compulsory for our franchisees to come to one of 19 separate training events over the next three months. We invoked a clause in the franchise agreement that said they had to come to one of these training events.

The first 18 of those events were great. In truth, what happened was they got less and less good the further down the line we went, because the people that came for the early events were the ones that were the most excited and enthused by the new offering. They were the ones most keen to embrace everything new. Whereas those who hated what we were doing or were in shock by it put off coming to the training. The last event was basically all those people who only came because if they didn't, they knew we were going to terminate their franchise agreement. There were only 30 of them, but it was a horrible event, full of negativity and misery.

The attitude of the whole group was wrong. There was huge resistance to what we were doing. There was even hatred, to some extent, turned on me, because we were implementing such a big change.

It took more than two years for the fallout from The Power of One to settle down. Over those two years we lost about a third of the franchisees who were at The Power of One that day. Some jumped; some were pushed.

Fortunately, it has all filtered through now and on the back of what was relaunched that day, we've now got dozens of our franchisees earning six-figure incomes from their business and providing exceptional and extraordinary services to businesses in their towns.

Clive Hannis in Gloucester and Simon Bullingham in Cheltenham were two franchisees in particular who took The Power of One offering and supercharged it. They came back at us several weeks later with a whole bunch of other ideas to really take their business onto another level yet again, and we still work very closely with them. They have both won our Franchisee of the Year Award over the last two to three years.

Complete Opposites

There was one notable absentee at The Power of One event, a guy named Andy Hurst. In the middle of June 2007, I concluded negotiations and had appointed Andy as my new Managing Director. I took advice from Denise Friend, who's my ace accountant (the one I upgraded to!). She's someone I turn to for advice on all the significant decisions that happen in my business because she's a very wise lady. She and her husband Malcolm are the senior partners in Birmingham's top accountancy and commercial finance firm, Friend LLP. Denise has been very supportive and very helpful to me over the years. I was talking to her early in 2007 about all the responsibility I was feeling.

I had a large business, I was employing over 30 staff, we had more than 300 franchisees, I now had four young children, a wife, and all these people were all hugely dependent on me.

The weight of responsibility was pretty heavy on my shoulders around that time. I felt a real desire to share that burden in some way, so on the back of some conversations with Denise, I commissioned a head-hunter and it took them three months to get me a shortlist of candidates to be my new MD. They cost me a fortune and what we set out to do was to get the person with the right personality and style, because I knew enough to know that what I didn't want was another one of me in the business!

What I was after was someone who was the complete opposite of me, so he or she would be brilliant at all the things that I'm rubbish at and vice-versa. I interviewed the candidates in June, just before The Power of One event, and Andy was head and shoulders ahead of all the others. He came to my house on a Saturday morning to finalise the negotiations and agree to his package. He couldn't actually join the business until October, because he had to work out quite a lengthy notice period with his current employer, hence he missed The Power of One, but he was instrumental in steering us through the choppy waters that came in its aftermath.

Andy has full responsibility for the day-to-day running of the business. I gave him my office and my PA. All my staff reported to him. I actually moved out and rented an office half a mile away on a completely different site, so I was able to get completely away from the day-to-day running of the business.

I've been liberated since his arrival. He takes care of all the things I'm not very good at and don't like doing. Having him has freed me up to be able to devote my energies and my time to things that I enjoy doing and that I'm best at. His arrival has been a big plus on many fronts.

I'm delighted with all the support I've been able to get from having a Managing Director. It's enabled us to build from those early foundations and really put down roots because we have someone who's very solid and sustainable. Andy's another key member of the team who has played a very big part in what has happened over the last three years.

CHAPTER 7
RARING2GO!

When you start to have a little bit of success in business, people start to find you. They start to seek you out. For a number of years now, at least two or three times a month, somebody will approach me with an idea or proposition.

Either they want me to invest in something or they want me to promote something via our thebestof network. I'll be honest: most of the things that have been brought to me have been rubbish, but occasionally something good does come out of these ideas. Nowadays, if people send me stuff unsolicited I won't even look at it, let alone reply, unless they're especially creative or are introduced to me via someone I know. (I'm not being rude, but just because you've sent me something that I didn't ask for and isn't very good, doesn't obligate me to spend time replying to you.)

Over the next two chapters, I want to talk about a couple of instances where I've been approached. One story is a successful one and the other one isn't!

Sally and Kirsten

Let's start in 2006. Sally Frost was a lady who had initially bought one of our very early My Mag Packs, and then she came to the Secret Meeting and in the summer of 2005 had invested in thebestof, buying the franchise for Wolverhampton in the West Midlands.

She brought in someone to help her run thebestof Wolverhampton – her friend, Kirsten Williams. In the spring of 2006 Sally emailed, asking if she and Kirsten could come to see me because they had something they thought I might be interested in. Since I knew Sally well, I invited her to Solihull. They came along and brought a little magazine they'd produced called *Raring2Go!* Essentially, it was positioned as the definitive guide to what to do with your kids in and around Wolverhampton.

I liked it a lot. It was full of things to do and places to go with children. They told me that they were delivering this magazine through school bookbags. I was really quite taken with this. They'd been running it for almost a year, alongside both thebestof and Sally's My Mag, and it was working very well. It was also proving very profitable for them.

They felt it could be franchised out. They explained that they weren't equipped to do that, but they knew I was and they were seeking an agreement that would work for both of us and see *Raring2Go!* scaled up as a franchise.

So, we came to an agreement there and then. They signed over all intellectual property rights to us, and in turn we would pay them a generous commission on every franchise that was sold. All the back-end/residual income would be ours.

They were heavily involved in building the franchise model. They did a lot of the work and of course their existing magazine served as the pilot. The magazine would be produced by the franchisee. To support it, we put in place a centralised website, so all the content from all the magazines across the country were amalgamated onto the website. The magazines would go out three or four times a year to coincide with the main school holidays. The magazines would be delivered through school bookbags and because it targeted a particular niche – i.e., young primary schoolchildren – we thought this would work very well.

It fit well with our existing brands. Because My Mag was a magazine and thebestof was still just a website at that point, *Raring2Go!* was a hybrid of the two, so to speak. We were able to leverage our capabilities with their concepts and the result was the launch of our second franchise in September 2006.

There were a number of things we had to fix to make this work. The first was to be sure that our franchisees would be able to get their magazines distributed through schools. This actually turned out to be one of the easiest things to do. Primary schools have a whole host of targets that they have to meet. These targets are set by the Department of Education, and the schools are expected to comply with and meet those targets. One such target was for the schools to be able to demonstrate they were playing a part in the local community. By distributing our *Raring2Go!* magazines, they did that because there were articles and content as well as promotions for businesses that were in the local area providing services for children. This allowed the schools to tick that box.

As long as you had the right conversation with the right person at the school, it was very straightforward. I remember a *Raring2Go!* franchisee in Birmingham managed to secure distribution through schools of over 60,000 magazines in just one week. That's how easy it was and how quick it was to build a very large-scale distribution. This gave our franchisees great leverage with local child-oriented businesses because we were delivering their message direct to their audience with no waste. It was beautiful.

Managing the Print

With our My Mag business, My Maggers had been able to get their magazines printed locally wherever they wanted. We realised if *Raring2Go!* was to become a national brand, then we'd have to retain control over the print. So it was important that we found the right print partners. We were able to take some soundings from existing My Maggers and people that we knew were printing a lot of My Mag magazines.

We entered into conversations with Steve Rowland and Freddie St George, who were the directors of Evon Print, based in Sussex. We were very impressed with Steve and Freddie. They were very innovative and helped us pull the model and print processes together. They introduced some really great tools that would help with print management and would help ensure that not only would our franchisees get a great-looking magazine, but it would also save them a lot of time and money in the process.

We signed a contract with them where they would become the printer for all the *Raring2Go!* magazines. Within 12 months, we were printing over a million magazines each term. It got very big, very quickly.

Of course, some franchisees struggled. A few saw *Raring2Go!* as a short cut to wealth and riches, but they didn't want to do the work. Of course, it's activity and action that builds a business, not dreams and plans, so these people came unstuck. There's no business that we've been involved in that you can build successfully if you are sitting behind your desk. You need to be out there doing things, and that's certainly the case with *Raring2Go!*

Rapid Expansion and Fab Franchisees

We managed to sell a lot of *Raring2Go!* franchises quickly. We got to 100 within nine months. I had Stuart Bevins running it at this point, and also Paul Chapman, who had recently joined my team. I hired another franchisee development manager, a lovely lady called Trish Holder. She was a really great addition to the team and it helped because she was a mum. She was a very calming influence on a number of franchisees because she could relate to all aspects of their lives.

Our *Raring2Go!* franchisees were predominantly women. Not exclusively so, but the majority were. We had everyone from single mums to proper left-wing feminist activists. It was a very eclectic mix, with some fantastic people in there.

One fantastic franchisee was Maria, who was a single mum. She worked full time as a nurse in Ipswich, and she's built an amazing business with *Raring2Go!* working in between her shifts at the hospital. I remember talking to her on the phone one day. I was in London having a photo shoot done for some thebestof promotional stuff, and she told me, 'I'm sitting in the park, Nigel. The sun is shining, I have my laptop on my knee and I'm making money, thanks to you.'

Of course, what she said wasn't exactly true. Sure, we'd given her the opportunity, but the reason she was sat in the park making money was all down to her. She did the work, made the effort and had the drive to get the results. She really did develop her business very well and, as far as I'm aware, she continues to thrive to this day.

Another big success story in *Raring2Go!* was Victoria Drysdale, who bought the franchise for Aberdeen. She's a very switched-on lady, really quite formidable, and she built a very sizable business very quickly with *Raring2Go!* For a long time, she was our star franchisee. Her magazines were thicker than everyone else's and her profits much larger.

We had a number of national advertisers in *Raring2Go!* Haven Holidays did very well as did the Merlin Group. They run Alton Towers, Warwick Castle and Madame Tussaud's, and they couldn't get enough of *Raring2Go!* They were very open about the fact that *Raring2Go!* was the best performing marketing they'd ever done.

One of the best campaigns we ran for them was for Alton Towers. We printed vouchers in the magazines (at no cost to them) and we then earned a small payment for every voucher that was redeemed. It worked very well for everybody. Our readers saved a ton of cash on entrance fees, we earned way more than we would have done just by selling the space and the Merlin Group got a far bigger and more cost effective response than with traditional advertising.

We got into bed with the Orlando Tourism Board and Virgin Holidays and that also worked well. Having these big national names was okay because most of the content in the magazines was local. We got the balance right.

What You See Isn't Always what You Get

As with any new business, there were one or two challenges in the beginning, including some things that, with hindsight, we didn't handle as well as we should have and that caused unnecessary anxiety and stress among franchisees. One incident was around the front cover. We wanted to put something on the front cover without realising just how proud our franchisees were of their front covers and how much they coveted that space. It caused a massive row and lots of bad feeling. It was a mistake and poor judgement on my part. We sorted it

Botty's Rule No. 15
Make money or make excuses
– but you can't do both.

In thebestof, dozens of franchisees are making six-figure incomes, but we've also got people doing much less. Every day my franchisee development team receives requests for assistance. Some of these calls are, frankly, whinges. Which franchisees do you think they come from?

We never get any whinges from our top 20% of franchisees. They're too busy making money. The people that make excuses are invariably the ones who are not making money.

Last year we surveyed over 1,000 businesses. One of the questions was:

'What's the single biggest obstacle stopping your business from growing this year?'

Amazingly, one of the top three answers was 'the government'.

Now this isn't about politics, it's about your mindset. Let's get one thing straight: if you catch yourself thinking that the government is the biggest obstacle to the growth of your business, you are screwed! Hand over the keys and go and do something else because you will never be super-successful in business.

It's our job as entrepreneurs to thrive despite what happens in Westminster.

In fact, excuses don't have to come out of your mouth. They can live, quite happily, eating away at your success levels in your head. It's as much about what you think as it's about what you say.

out, but it was painful when it needn't have been. To those franchisees reading this who were around at that time – sorry.

We found out a number of our franchisees were being two-faced with us. They'd be on the phone saying quite nice things to us or when we'd meet them, they were very pleasant, but then we uncovered a hidden forum online where they were saying some very different things that were not only uncomplimentary but very unfair and untrue.

So, the lesson I learnt is that what you see with people in business isn't always what you get. I'm very straightforward and open. You always know where you stand with me and if I've got a problem or an issue, I'll tell you. Not everyone is like that, of course, and I think we were perhaps a little too trusting in those early days. We also assumed that everyone shared the same values and integrity as us, but sadly that isn't always the case, either.

We had one or two amusing run-ins as well during that time with our franchisees. The franchisees were the editors of their own magazines. That meant that they could put articles in the magazine, and we encouraged them to do this. The articles had to be relevant to the audience. This is a magazine aimed at the parents of children under nine, and being distributed through school bookbags, don't forget. We retained right of approval over any and all content in their magazine. They had to come to us for approval prior to going to print so we could ensure the integrity of the brand.

One day, a magazine came through and the main feature on the front cover and the biggest article inside was a story all about underaged sex. It was completely inappropriate for a *Raring2Go!* magazine. But the franchisee didn't see it that way. She refused to withdraw it and we had to use our rights to veto the article which caused a lot of bad feelings and damaged our relationship with that particular franchisee (although it helped us with many other franchisees, and it's always helpful when people know that you're prepared to use your power!)

The website was an issue for some franchisees. What we saw was the same pattern emerging with *Raring2Go!* that we'd experienced with thebestof. The people that whinge and whine and make excuses are never, ever the people that are making the money. What I've learnt to be true is that you can either make excuses in business or you can make money, but you cannot do both; excuses and making money are completely incompatible.

We had lots of franchisees making good money, building big businesses and publishing fantastic magazines – those people never complained about the website, or anything else for that matter, but others used the website as an excuse and their businesses were diminished as a result.

In any franchise network where you have a spread of performers, from your top performers to your bottom performers, what you'll find is that the people towards the lower end will be the most vocal at making excuses and blaming everything on everyone other than themselves.

On thebestof, we had a forum that our franchisees could use. We found it was becoming very well used, to the point where some people were on there such a lot that it was hard to see how they could be doing any work. We did a bit of analysis and found that of our top 20 most prolific forum users, 14 of that top 20 were in our bottom 10% of performers. Interesting, eh! (And yes, I did shout about and use that stat a lot to shame people into better behaviours and focus!)

Nurture ... and Reduce Costs!

We had our first national conference for *Raring2Go!* around 18 months after launch. It got everything back on track. It showed us the importance of communication. You can send regular emails out and do podcasts and other forms of communication, but actually nothing is better or more effective than sitting down and talking face-to-face to people.

That's what we did there. We invested some money, bought the rights to a Robbie Williams track and put a DVD together. We gave them a portable DVD player to help them sell, because some of the franchisees were having trouble doing that. We basically put the sales pitch on a DVD and our instructions were to go to the businesses, explain to them that you have something really exciting and interesting to share with them, put the DVD on and shut up. It worked.

We were also able to reduce the costs for our franchisees. Print costs were coming down. Printing was generally still very highly priced in the UK compared to overseas, but our colleagues at Evon Print were able to reduce their prices and we passed all those savings on to our franchisees to help make their businesses more successful and profitable.

Throughout this time, the *Raring2Go!* network was continuing to grow. The number of magazines was growing, the website was growing and, the number of businesses that were featured was growing. It was a very positive and healthy situation and the outlook was good.

An Offer I Couldn't Refuse

One day in October 2008, Steve and Freddie from Evon Print came to see me and Andy Hurst in Solihull, where they made me an offer I couldn't refuse. They wanted to take on the *Raring2Go!* business. They obviously knew it very well because they'd been so heavily involved in everything that we'd done. It was interesting to see their logic. What they saw through *Raring2Go!* is that the quarterly print runs of the magazines, if they were able to secure that business for the long term, would effectively enable them to cover a very large portion of their overhead for the rest of their business. It gave them certainty. In addition, they had also identified further enhancements and developments that they could profitably make to the business. By investing in and taking on *Raring2Go!*, they were able to not only develop it more fully, but also secure the core Evon Print business.

It was strange selling something that we'd built from scratch – but it was undoubtedly the right thing to do for everyone involved, including our franchisees. The transaction was completed in February 2009 and *Raring2Go!* continues to flourish and thrive to this day.

I'm very pleased and proud to have played a key part in the development of *Raring2Go!* To a very large extent, we realised the vision that Sally and Kirsten had first articulated to me just over two years previously. We built it into a national brand with national coverage and a big network. It was incredibly fulfilling for them, as well as for us.

CHAPTER 8
HAVE A QUICKIE

In many ways, some of my biggest lessons in business have come from my experience with Quickie. It all started when I got a call from one of my thebestof franchisees who was running the thebestof Leicester at the time. His name is David Heath. He was a former Great Britain athlete, a middle-distance runner, and he'd also been a very successful My Magger, building up an extremely profitable local magazine business.

He did a bit of work for us helping to train My Maggers – which he was very good at. Whenever I spent time with David, it was enjoyable. He was just a really great guy who had a cracking attitude to life and to business. So, when he rang and asked if he could show me something, I didn't hesitate to invite him down.

The Concept

David came and met me at my house one afternoon with a huge holdall which he kept closed at the beginning of the meeting. He explained that he had secured the UK rights to a product that he believed was going to cause a real storm across the country.

He told me that it was a business that had a twin revenue stream and he felt it would work really well. He unzipped the holdall, and he pulled out this machine, which looked like a very large mobile phone. It sat about two feet high, and in the middle of it was a 10-inch TV screen. Underneath the TV screen there were a lot of wires hanging out with sockets on the ends.

He explained that this was a mobile phone charger – with a difference. It charged mobile phones very quickly. It didn't give a trickle charge like your standard chargers do, instead it was able to give most phones an 80% charge in 10 minutes.

His concept was that people would put a one-pound coin in the machine, plug their phone into the appropriate lead and then get this fast charge. Perfect when you were caught short of battery power and you were out and about.

I can certainly relate to having been stuck somewhere with a dead phone or one that was dying. In that situation, the ability to get a quick charge in a few minutes for a pound would be very attractive.

He then explained the second revenue stream from his machine: the TV screen could play adverts. Because people were likely to stay around the machine for 10 minutes (after all, their mobile phone was plugged into it – they weren't going to wander very far), he reasoned that they would watch the screen. This created a great opportunity to promote businesses, so the advertising on the screen could be sold and the revenue from the machines would be a great business. It was a double whammy – revenue from the one-pound charges, and revenue from the advertising, and a product that lots of people would need and use.

David sold it very well to me and one of the key parts was that he'd come up with this great name for the business. 'Nige, we're going to call it "Quickie".' he explained.

'The signage could say something like, "Have a Quickie",

or "Get a Quickie here",' he went on. He convinced me that it would all work very well.

He continued to explain how he had secured exclusive distributorship on these particular machines in the UK. But he had no money to fulfil his obligations under that distributorship agreement, and he had to buy a whole load of these machines within the next three months or he would lose those rights, so he was coming to me to seek my investment in this business.

Into Partnership

I liked David; I'd known him for three years. I thought he had something worthwhile here. I made the decision to invest in his business, and we set up a new company. He called it Quickie Products Limited, and we split the shares 50/50. I was really busy at this point and had little time to spare on anything new. My Mag was still thriving, thebestof was going well and *Raring2Go!* was underway. I wasn't looking for something else to do with my time, so the deal was that I would put the money in, and he would do the work. Effectively, I was an investor in the business.

He ordered the chargers, I wrote a cheque for £64,000, and the Quickie machines started to come over from China. As he began to roll them out, they were really successful. The advertising was working well – and the takings from the machines themselves were also ahead of what we had expected – especially those that David sited in hotels or busy bars. David was good at going out and securing sites for the machines. He was also very good, given his background with thebestof and with My Mag, at securing advertising for the machines as well. It was looking good.

'We Should Franchise This …'

After a couple of months, he came to me and suggested that we should franchise the business. He knew I understood franchising and he talked to me about how it would allow us to expand rapidly without significant further investment. He had identified, rightly, that it would take years for him to build national coverage working on his own and that if we were to recruit a sales force, that would require a further six-figure investment. Perhaps N5, he suggested, could help sell the franchises as an agent of Quickie Products. Meanwhile, he would run the business and train and take care of the franchisees once they came on board.

It was an interesting idea. We would market and sell the franchises on behalf of Quickie Products. Quickie would pay N5 an agency fee from each sale. The franchisees would keep all the cash from their machines and all the revenue from advertising, and they would pay a fixed monthly fee, per machine, to Quickie Products. David would run all aspects of the Quickie business, including sourcing and maintaining the machines and training and supporting the franchisees.

The model in that respect is entirely logical, and it should have worked really well. But it didn't. Fairly quickly, problems started to emerge.

Problems and Problems

The first issue arose when the initial wave of machines needed updating. These were the original machines that we had acquired only weeks earlier but the phone manufacturers had introduced new charging sockets, so they needed to be upgraded. iPods had started becoming popular at about this time as well (although it was long before the iPhone) and we had no iPod charging leads on the machines. They needed to be installed, as we were getting a lot of requests for these, especially from gyms that had the machines.

Updating the leads wasn't a difficult job and we'd been aware of the changes that were coming, but it proved much harder than it should have been to get the new leads from China. It was a lot of hassle, and it took much longer than it should have. Soon after dealing with that, a bigger problem occurred when we took delivery of our next batch of machines from China, only to find that they were not charging properly. Rather than getting an 80% charge in 10 minutes, they were only delivering something like 20–30% in 10 minutes. Not much of a Quickie!

Reports started getting back to me of poor support and service to franchisees from the Quickie operations team. New franchisees were experiencing long delays getting their machines, which I couldn't understand. The process was simple: new franchisee comes on board, machines ordered, machines delivered. But this wasn't happening. The whole supply side was going wrong.

At this point, David had moved his family to France and was working from there. He was commuting to the UK most weeks, but this was not an ideal situation, to say the least. N5 wasn't getting paid by Quickie for the work that it was doing on the sales and marketing of the franchise, and we were out of pocket by over £50,000.

I called a meeting with David. It was clear to me that Quickie needed a new machine design that would cope with all these new leads, and was also able to charge phones and iPods properly. This was something that I knew nothing about. It was also apparent that, despite my initial investment, Quickie needed significantly more cash in order to fund it properly. The franchise fees were all being spent on acquiring new machines, and I wasn't prepared to invest any further money at that point.

I decided to resign to allow David to find another investor. If I stepped aside, I reasoned, then it would allow him to bring someone else into the business who would be knowledgeable in the right areas, who would have the right expertise and who would be able to fund the business appropriately.

A Six-Figure Loss

I knew that by resigning I was almost certainly going to have a big loss. I wanted Quickie to succeed but to do so, it needed new blood, new investment and new expertise – none of which I could provide. What I could do was write-off the money owed to me and walk away. I was already beginning to regret getting involved in a partnership in the first place and I certainly wasn't enjoying it. Although I liked David and respected him, he didn't run Quickie in the way that I would have done, so I left.

David did secure another investor fairly quickly who came on board and injected a big chunk of cash into the business as well as buying my shares. I took a huge loss. Suffice to say that the combination of the loss on the shares and the unpaid invoices to N5 came to a very sizeable six-figure sum.

I bowed out for a couple reasons. Firstly, I wanted to give Quickie every chance to flourish and succeed. While I was clear that I didn't want to be part of it going forward, the concept was still sound and with the right management it ought to be able to thrive, I believed. But that probably wasn't going to happen if I put pressure on Quickie to pay what it owed me or N5, which is why it was all written-off.

Botty's Rule No. 16
S**t happens – and it always will.

How you cope with setbacks will be the making of you.
I've been fortunate. I haven't really had any major catastrophes in my life, not like those that some people have had to contend with. But I've had more than my fair share of setbacks in business and Quickie was certainly one of them.

There have been other things that haven't gone to plan, either: large bad debts, unexpected tax bills, staff that have stolen from me, people that have ripped me off or copied my ideas. It's part of life. Bad things will always happen from time to time, so it's best to expect them, plan for them (where you can), but most of all, make sure that you've got the right attitude, the right support system and network and the right people around you to ensure that when bad things do happen, you are able to bounce back quickly.

The more you study successful people, the more you'll discover how they don't have the Midas touch. No one does. Richard Branson has had his share of setbacks – he even spent a night in the cells back in 1969! My great idol, Walt Disney, was bankrupted before he ever enjoyed success with the first Mickey Mouse cartoons.

Wherever you find success, you'll find people who have overcome failure. You learn a lot about success from experiencing a few failures. I can definitely vouch for that.

The second reason I did it this way is that it enabled me to move on with no baggage or distractions – and with a clear conscience. I'd done all I could to help Quickie, but it hadn't turned out as I'd hoped. It was never meant to consume any of my time. I was just an investor. But in the final few weeks of my involvement, I'd spent hours each day trying to fix Quickie, to the detriment of my core business, N5. Now I could refocus all my energies on N5, and that was worth a great deal to me. The Quickie loss was a price worth paying, painful though it was.

Unfortunately, 18 months after I resigned as a director and left the business, Quickie went into liquidation. I know that I lost more money on Quickie than anybody else, but I also know that other people, franchisees mainly, also lost money on it, and I feel very bad about that.

Ultimately, we all take responsibility for our decisions in life. No one that came on board with Quickie was forced to do so. We were very open and honest with everything on

Quickie, and I have no doubt that David did all he could, along with the new director and the investors, to make it a success. But it wasn't to be, and in that respect Quickie ranks right up at the top as one of my biggest failures in business.

The Quickie failure taught me a number of things. One of them is that entrepreneurs are typically attracted by bright, new, shiny objects and when it came to Quickie, I was no exception. When David came to pitch it to me, I was very excited by it as a business, but I really should have gone nowhere near it. Not because it wasn't good, but because I already had three businesses at that point, and I couldn't afford the dilution of focus. I was running My Mag, thebestof and *Raring2Go!*, all of which had huge potential and needed a lot of focus and energy. Taking on Quickie meant that I had to divert some of my focus away from my main brands. It wasn't so much about switching horses, but trying to ride another horse in the same race. If I'd been able to give Quickie my focus from the beginning, then maybe it would have had a different outcome – but I couldn't have done that because the other three brands needed my complete dedication.

The second lesson from Quickie was that partnerships are not for me. I need to be in full control. I had no control in Quickie. I was an investor, David was the Managing Director, and when I saw things I wasn't happy about, it was difficult. I could influence David, but ultimately he was the one who made the final decisions. It was his business, and I didn't enjoy that.

The third lesson is one that I should have learnt from my experience with the quiz machines many years earlier. Why would I want to go into a market that I didn't understand? Quickie was in a market/sector that I knew nothing about. I went in blind, which was stupid. It was the last time ever that I will invest in anything that I don't understand properly.

The fourth lesson is that you have to choose your people carefully. David is a great guy. My respect for him is considerable, but he was overstretched with Quickie. It's very different running a My Mag or thebestof as a franchisee to becoming the Managing Director of a live network and managing a whole lot of franchisees and logistics and operations, and perhaps the job was too big for David.

The final lesson I took from Quickie is that it's much better to invest in yourself and your ideas than investing it in other people. That's something that I carry on now, to this day. I'm very reluctant and resistant to investing my money and, certainly, any of my time and energy in anything that isn't part of our stable and that's come from within. As a result, I've turned down a heck of a lot of opportunities that have come across my desk in the last few years because of what I learnt from Quickie.

CHAPTER 9
MY LITTLE WRAPPER

When My Mag had begun to flourish, and we started to give some thought as to where our business was going, Sue suggested that we should introduce a personalised chocolate wrapping business in the UK. It was a market that we were familiar with from our many trips to America but which was untapped and pretty much unheard of in the UK. Sue thought that it would make a great product, very much in the mould of My Mag, and that we could market and sell it as a business opportunity.

We did a little bit of investigation into some of the US businesses to understand how they worked, but it became pretty clear that the biggest opportunity for us to focus our energies on at that time was thebestof and not any kind of chocolate-based business. So, we put it to one side and, I'll be honest with you, almost forgot about the idea that there may be some opportunity there. We ignored it for over three years.

In the spring of 2008, Andy Hurst, my Managing Director, had got his feet properly under the desk, and I'd been freed up and liberated to do the stuff I enjoyed doing, which was creating new products and new businesses. The idea of creating a new market in the UK for personally wrapped chocolate bars was something that I thought was attractive; doubly so because, by this point, we were also generating an awful lot of leads and interest in My Mag that we couldn't fulfil. Remember, when someone bought a My Mag Pack from us, they bought the rights to distribute within a specific postcode area, so we couldn't sell that postcode to anyone else. The upshot was that My Mag had been so popular and so successful that we were running out of areas to sell. We still had all these leads. Every week dozens of people were getting in touch with us wanting to buy a My Mag Pack. Typically, they were stay-at-home mums who were looking to work part time from home.

These people were looking for a home-based business, and it seemed a shame that we had nothing to sell them. I was quite driven to come up with something else that would meet their needs and obviously allow us to make the most of the opportunities. I decided to give this chocolate business a whirl. We refreshed all our research, and set off to build the business and get it launched in the UK. I gave myself a deadline of six weeks.

Our research in the UK had shown that this was pretty much a completely untapped market. Obviously, chocolate is very popular, but getting personalised chocolate was really not easy to do at all. You could buy in bulk, with companies that would do 500 or 1,000 bars, but there was nowhere that was providing any product that would work for children's birthday parties or weddings.

What we wanted to produce was beautifully wrapped chocolate with the wrapper personalised for the occasion. These bars are brilliant in party bags. It might have a nice little personalised design that says, for example, 'Tabitha is 9!' on the front, and on the back, 'Thanks for coming to my party. I hope you had a great time, Love Tabitha xx'. There could even be a little photograph on there.

I knew there was potential in the corporate market as well. For professional service companies, it's great to have small chocolate bars, personalised to their brand and logo, in their

Botty's Rule No. 17
Give customers the chance to buy a premium-priced product.

In most businesses, 20% of customers will pay more for a premium product or service IF you make it available to them.

In all walks of life, there are plenty of examples of businesses offering premium levels of product or service. Theatre tickets, airfares, hotels – they all have different levels of price that people can choose to pay. Yet it is much more unusual to find premium products or services in small businesses. Implementing this in your business can, however, generate a double-digit percentage increase in profit *immediately*, as I found out with My Little Wrapper.

When we introduced My Little Wrapper, we initially only had a single product. Three months in, however, we introduced a Professional Pack to the range. The Professional Pack sold for 50% more, but generated almost 100% more gross margin. Purchasers get a lot more stuff but it's a more profitable product for us. The only thing we changed with our marketing and sales was that when a customer rang up to buy, we said, 'That's great, would you like the Standard Pack or the Professional Pack?' That's all we did. We didn't change any of our ads, it wasn't even on the website, but we asked the question when people came in to buy. From the first month when we did it, right up to the current day, every single month between 19%–21% of our customers buy the Professional Pack.

I had a chiropractor who said this couldn't possibly apply to his business. He was wrong. He now has different prices for his appointments depending on the time of day. If you want to see him first thing in the morning or in the early evening, then you pay a premium price. His lunchtime prices are also more expensive than his standard price. If you want to pay the lower price, you can, but you have to see him between 9 a.m. and noon or between 2 p.m. and 5 p.m. He's introduced premium pricing to reflect the time of day and the result has been an increase in his profits of over 20% in the last 12 months for exactly the same amount of work – and he's lost no clients.

Every business has the opportunity to introduce a premium product or service. Drycleaners do it, my local taxi company does it (you can pay £5 extra and get a 'gold car' (i.e., a slightly more up-to-date and cleaner vehicle than the usual eight-year-old Nissan Bluebird!). It's there for everyone. What's your premium price offering?

receptions. They are also fab as part of a product launch or at exhibitions. The bars work well for charity fundraising. They're personalised for the charity, who acquire them whole-sale and then sell them in their shops and at their events.

In short, there was clearly a market for this to work. We knew that there were thousands of people looking to work part time from home and this would be a great thing for them to do, so I hunkered down and set about creating it.

Six Weeks …

I announced to the whole team at N5 that I would emerge in six weeks' time with a product that we were able to sell. The first thing I did was schedule the event that I'd use to launch it, book the venue and email 50,000 prospective franchisees to tell them to keep the date clear because we'd be launching something exciting that day. That made my deadline immovable and would ensure that I knuckled down and got the work done. It's a neat tactic and very effective. I use it regularly, and I've never missed a deadline yet!

I Need Chocolate … and I Need It Now!

One of the things we had to decide quite early on was who was going to supply our chocolate to us. You can't legally rewrap commercially available chocolate bars. We couldn't, for instance, suggest that our clients bought Kit Kats, took off their wrappers and rewrap them in their branded livery. That would cause all sorts of problems, not just with food and hygiene regulations but also from a copyright, branding and trademark perspective. I delegated the task of finding our chocolate supplier to one of my team who had asked me if she could get involved with the project. I gave her four days and asked for at least three options for me to choose from. On the fourth day she came to see me and told me she couldn't find anything – not one single UK supplier of chocolate bars that met our (very flexible) brief. I was extremely disappointed. She had been really keen to work closely with me on projects and making new things happen; she seemed really driven but it turned out she hadn't got the nous or the initiative for this type of work. It was a big let-down for me.

I jumped online (ain't Google wonderful!) and was able to source the chocolate pretty quickly. Within two days, I had a number of different options and was able to come to a deal with a manufacturer. It wasn't difficult. Getting the chocolate sorted early in the project was very, very important because we were going to wrap these chocolate bars, so the wrappers had to precisely fit the chocolate. It would be a lot easier to change the wrapper size than to change the chocolate bar sizes. So by using existing moulds, I was able to get the chocolate sourced and then develop the wrapper sizes to fit the chocolate.

I did involve one other member of my team in quite some depth in developing the product. She was energised and enthusiastic. I involved her right from the word go, and she did a great job. I also invited all the team at N5 to come up with a name for the new business. Our lead developer on the tech team, John Price, came up with the name My Little Wrapper and won himself a bottle of champagne and a small place in history. Thanks, John.

It's a Wrap

We were going to offer a business-in-a-box and that meant we had to think of everything and work it all through in great detail. Our customers would buy a My Little Wrapper Pack and with that they would have everything needed to set up their own personalised chocolate-wrapping business. There would be, first of all, some chocolate. We had two sizes of chocolate bars: small (10g) and medium (40g) bars.

Next, we'd provide them with the wrappers – all of which were professionally designed. I commissioned three designers to come up with a suite of wrapper designs, including one guy who had previously designed all the Cadbury's chocolate wrappers for the previous 20 years, including brands like Flake. For launch, we had 71 different wrapper designs. There are now over 100.

The wrappers are all preprinted with the core themes and designs and our Wrapper people then overprint the personalisation. We provide them with some whizzy software, which enables them to add the personalisation on each wrapper in exactly the right place. They would overprint the personalisation on their home printer and we specified the particular printer they'd use that would work with the paper on the wrapper.

Because we went to this level of detail, we were able to get nice wrapper paper so it looks like a proper chocolate wrapper, with the right gloss and sheen. If you try and wrap chocolate in normal copier paper, for instance, you'll see how rubbish it looks. So we had to source the paper, as well as the printer and the wrappers ... and make sure the wrappers would fold and crease nicely around the bars.

Along with supplying the chocolate, the wrappers and the software to do the personalisation, we also supplied the marketing materials so that our customers – the people who were running the business in their local area – had all the different collateral (postcards, flyers, leaflets, etc.) that they needed to get their customers. We provided a whole set of marketing materials, techniques and tools to help them.

Cameron's Starring Role

So that was how the puzzle all came together. For the first time in business, I worked with my eldest son, Cameron, who was 12 years old at the time. We used Cameron in the training videos that we produced to show people how to wrap the chocolate bars. Obviously, when someone overprints the wrappers, they go through the printer as an A4 sheet, and they then need cutting, so we supplied a cutter with the My Little Wrapper Pack. Cameron showed on video how easy it was to cut the wrappers to size, wrap the chocolate, glue the wrapper and then package the whole thing up.

He really enjoyed doing it, and he became quite a well-known character within the business. A lot of the purchasers really warmed to his, how shall we say, unique style. His age turned out to be a great line for us because we were able to use it in our marketing. 'It's so easy to do, even a 12-year-old can do it.' He enjoyed it, and it helped with the positioning of the business as well. I very generously paid him £50 for his work, and he learnt a valuable lesson about negotiation and image rights!

The Men in Murmansk

A Russian company developed the software for us. It was our first foray into outsourcing software development overseas. My core tech team under the very capable leadership of Nigel Davis were building the new website for the thebestof during 2008, so I didn't want to deflect them onto this new product. I wanted it done as a stand-alone project. It was a real lesson for me, just in terms of how easy it is to outsource work effectively to very well-qualified and capable people, if you know what you're doing. Nigel Davis brought invaluable expertise to the business in helping make this happen, and we've done it a number of times since – and each time has been very successful.

As the launch date approached, an interesting thing happened. I'd been using a local print shop for all our in-house print requirements. I'd been using them pretty much since the business started, so at this point, it was over five years. For some reason, the person working with me on this project went to another local print company to get a particular job done for our launch event. As a result of this, what came to light was that we appeared to have been significantly overcharged by our long-standing established print supplier. This really upset me because we'd been very loyal customers and the guy who ran the business had become quite good friends with me. I had seen him and his wife socially, and I was really disappointed because with a quick ring around, we started to get some quotes on the work that we were having done on a regular basis. It became pretty clear that we'd been paying way more then we should have been for quite a long time. Not just 3% or 5%, either, but 20%, 30%, even 50% in some instances. I felt quite aggrieved and thought I should have been better looked after than that.

You could argue that it was just me being naive. I never queried the prices we were charged, so why on earth would they want to reduce their price? The answer to that is because they lost my business for ever, as a result. We stopped all orders. We never told them we were stopping our orders – although I would have if they'd asked – we just started getting all our print through other local print companies. They never,

ever followed up with me. I never had a phone call, never had a piece of correspondence. Nothing. They must have known something had gone awry because we had spent a lot of money with them, but they never ever did anything about it once it stopped. Never even asked the question.

There are lessons from both sides here. I certainly should have been a lot more attentive to costs as my business expanded and grew. My response to needing to cover more costs was that I just needed to sell more stuff. We'd get on the front foot and generate more revenue. Whereas when Andy Hurst arrived in the business, he was able to get in and make some very significant savings – a five-figure monthly savings to our bottom line – just by getting proper control of the costs.

But there are also lessons from a supplier perspective because the outcome was clearly not satisfactory for that print company. Had they communicated with us and done something to try and win the business back, I probably would have tried them again. I would have been quite easy to get back if they'd handled it in the right way, but they made no attempt to do anything. It still seems very strange.

'They've Closed the Motorway'

Let's get back to the launch event for My Little Wrapper. We were able to go out with a big campaign to all the people that had enquired about My Mag in the previous four years. The message was basically along the lines of 'Nigel Botterill launches his next business venture … come along, and get a slice of the action.' The people that had bought into thebestof at the Secret Meetings right at the beginning got an incredible deal, and the implicit message was that you may get the same kind of deal if you come along to this event.

We just did this as a single event, and we hosted it at the Warwick Hilton, which is right in the middle of the country just off Junction 15 of the M40. We had 280 people booked, so we were very excited. I set off mid-afternoon to make sure all the preparations were in hand, and to be sure that everything was going to plan. Just as I got to the hotel, there was a very nasty accident on the motorway, and they ended up closing the M40 in both directions for three hours.

This was a disaster for us. Rather than the 280 people we were expecting, only 70 made it. The rest were stuck on the motorway and just couldn't get there. It was very, very disappointing, but we still managed to sell 25 My Little Wrapper Packs on day one – which more than covered all the development costs. It also meant that almost one in three people that did come to the event bought a pack. It was another great example of how selling 'one-to-many' and putting on events can be a very effective way of growing your business.

I just wish we'd had a room full of people on that day because the evidence suggests we could have shifted many more packs. Having said that, we followed up with everyone, and the growth of My Little Wrapper accelerated rapidly in the spring and summer of 2008.

More Pay-per-Click

As well as marketing to our database, the primary route by which we developed and sold My Little Wrapper was through Google AdWords pay-per-click. We have used pay-per-click for all of our businesses, not just My Little Wrapper. We'd used it extensively back in the early days of My Mag, and it had played a big part in the growth of thebestof and *Raring2Go!* as well. We'd become pretty expert at it; we studied a lot, tested everything and tracked our results religiously. One of the best things about pay-per-click is that it's very immediate and responsive.

You can turn it on and off at leisure, and, of course, you are only targeting your ads to people who are searching for whatever terms are appropriate; you can also tightly control your budgets.

I mentioned in an earlier chapter that I was keen to spend as much money as I could on pay-per-click because once I had it right, I was going to get a return that was many times greater than my investment. We were so prolific with our spend that I got invited on a couple of occasions across to Dublin to spend a day or two with Google at their European HQ. They looked after us royally and it was fascinating to get an inside track on how Google works and see some of the cool stuff that they were working on and trialling. It was also a great education for me. I learnt in great detail about how the search engine ranks pages and how pay-per-click works. What became apparent during my first visit, when I was part of a large group, was that what they'd done was invite their top 100 European customers. That meant I was paying them a lot of money, but when we started on pay-per-click back in 2004, we were, in many ways, pioneers, and those trips to Dublin were very educational … and they kept me spending!

Back in 2004, we were often the only people bidding for pay-per-click on many of our keywords. There was no competition, and we were paying only one or two pence per click. Things are quite different now, of course. It's used widely by many successful businesses. But most local businesses are still missing out because they're not engaged with and are not utilising pay-per-click. It is a very powerful marketing tool that all business owners ought to understand and know about.

Botty's Rule No. 18
Pay-per-Click – one of the most powerful business tools ever …

Without doubt, pay-per-click advertising has been the single biggest driver of sales into my business over the last seven years. I've used it to promote all our products, and I've spent, literally, millions of pounds with Google and it's been an absolute pleasure to do so. You see, every time I spend £1 with Google, I get £4, £5 or £6, sometimes as much as £10, back. It's like a little money-making machine, once you've worked out how to do it properly. I've spent over £143,000 with Google in a single month. I tell you that not to brag or boast, but to give you some indication of the size of the prize here. It's massive.

Now while it's true that pay-per-click has become much more competitive recently than it was in those heady days of 2003–04, it is still an extremely powerful tool. And you can control your budget precisely, so you know exactly what your return is on investment at any time. You can start small, with fairly modest budgets.

When you can crack pay-per-click (and for most local businesses it's relatively easy to do), it can advance your business forward very quickly.

If you don't understand how it works or you've never tried it, then stop reading now and, go to **www.nigel botterill.com/bookoffer**. Join my Entrepreneurs' Circle and do the online training in which I teach you how to use pay-per-click. It will enable you to get up and going with Google AdWords today. Do it properly, and that should ensure that you're putting money into your business and making sales by tomorrow.

It's also very easy to implement as long as you know what you're doing, and it is not difficult to learn.

With My Little Wrapper, we didn't give people any area exclusivity on the product. There was no restriction on where people could market or sell their bars. The reason for this is very simple: with the magazines it was all about distribution, so you could only distribute your magazines within your specific postcode area. However, you could get your advertisers from wherever you wanted to. The logic was simple: businesses would only advertise with you if your distribution area was relevant to them. With the personalised chocolate bars, there was no issue with distribution, so we didn't put any territory restrictions into the business whatsoever. We figured that people had contacts all over the country. People know friends and family in different towns, and they'd want to do business and sell to them. It would be wrong of us to try and restrict that in some way. Also, by not having any territories, we didn't limit our 'stock' of things to sell in the way that we'd inhibited the growth of My Mag as we ran out of postcode areas.

Commercial Stupidity and Eye off the Ball …

People pretty much had to buy their chocolate from us. They weren't compelled contractually to do so, but we knew it was very difficult to source chocolate bars that were exactly the same size as the ones that we were providing and, of course, our wrappers were all made for our size of chocolate bars. By far the easiest thing to do is to get them from us, which is what people did.

This meant we were quickly shipping over 40,000 chocolate bars each month. They were used for weddings, birthdays, corporate, charities, bar mitzvahs and a host of other events and parties. People loved 'em.

We expanded our range by introducing different sizes of bars and, as our wrapper clients requested them, we also introduced additional wrapper designs. They'd put a request in for a particular design, and if it was a sensible one and there was a market for it, we'd get it designed. We also made it available for everyone else to access as well.

On the face of it, My Little Wrapper was going very well, but about a year or so into the business, I started to pick up on my radar that maybe things weren't running quite as smoothly as they should be. I had a customer service team that looked after all our customers, our franchisees and our My Maggers, and they were also responsible for looking after My Little Wrapper after they'd bought the product.

During the summer of 2008, I started to get a few complaints. They were from people that I knew quite well because they were thebestof franchisees or they'd been My Maggers. I heard about chocolate and wrappers that had been ordered and not delivered or people saying they had asked for something four times and no one had called them back.

These were classic symptoms of poor customer service. When I began to investigate, what I discovered was really quite shocking. It caused me quite a bit of distress because when I took a day out to really get behind the scenes and find out what was going on, I uncovered some huge problems.

We were out of stock on chocolate, for instance, which is ridiculous. There was a written process (which I'd written!) to ensure we never ran out of chocolate, but it wasn't being followed. Wrappers were not stored in any kind of ordered way in our stockroom. I found that we'd ordered some new wrappers the previous day, and we'd ordered in a very small quantity. Now, with any kind of print, to get the price down per unit you have to order in a high volume. Wrappers were being ordered in small quantities, and so we were paying about nine times more to source the wrappers than we were actually charging our customers to buy them. So, as well as providing rubbish service – because there were delays every-where – we were losing money on quite some scale on the back-end of the My Little Wrapper business.

The people in my team who were responsible for this part of the business were not owning up to the problem. They were not doing their jobs properly and as far as I was concerned they were sabotaging my business.

The commercial stupidity on wrapper ordering, allied to the lack of organisation and adherence to processes, was clearly a real issue. I overheard one of my team in the office say that it wasn't her job to ship chocolate. I challenged her and she retorted that it also wasn't her responsibility to go and pack up some orders that had been received and send them to our customers. I went ballistic.

Botty's Rule No. 19
No one cares as much as you ...

Don't forget that – ever ...

There's a very big difference between people who start and build businesses – entrepreneurs – and those who work for them – employees. The truth is, we're a different breed.

And here's another truth: it is almost unheard of for a business owner to go through his or her entire business life with a single employee staying with him or her the whole time. It just doesn't happen. You will always be there after they have gone and no matter how much you like them or how much they like you or how committed they are and how 'they think of the business just like it's their own ...' at some point they will leave. Also, they have nothing invested in the business – not like you do.

My advice here is cautionary. Good staff are essential and they're hard to find. When you find one, you want to keep hold of him or her as long as you possibly can. But please don't ever confuse that with allowing yourself to think that your employees care for your business to the same extent you do. I'm not saying that they don't care – many do – it's just that they're not in the same ballpark as you.

As if that wasn't enough, I also uncovered some apparent systematic mis-selling of the product by the member of my team that had been working with me on the whole project from inception. When people were ringing up and asking for exclusivity in a particular area, she was giving it to them, and then not recording it anywhere and not telling any of her colleagues. Then somebody else would call to order, and we'd sell them a pack in their area and that would cause problems.

Back to the Floor …

I had to get to grips with all of these issues. I knew it was my business and my responsibility because ultimately the buck stops with me. I was being let down by a number of my staff and so, as a result of what I found, three staff left immediately. For two weeks I did everything. I became the store manager, the chocolate orderer, the packager, the shifter, the picker.

I organised everything. I got the storeroom kitted out properly and I made sure I understood exactly what was going on. With hindsight, it was something I should have done eight or nine months earlier when we'd launched the business. It would have been very helpful and would have saved a lot of heartache and grief if I'd immersed myself in the detail of the business at the beginning. I'd like to think that I didn't need to do that, but the thing is, no one else is going to care about my business as much as I do, and while I really relied on the people to do their jobs, they hadn't done them.

It took many months for me to spot that they had not been doing their jobs properly – many months of damage to my business.

I replaced those three staff with a single person. Kathy McEvoy joined me in October 2008 and she's been a real star addition to our team. She handles all the customer service on My Little Wrapper, and takes care of all our ordering and stock management and stock control. She's recently started taking on responsibility for the Entrepreneurs' Circle membership as well. Every business needs people like Kathy. I'm delighted that she's part of our team.

I decided to do all the interviews while I was doing the job I was hiring for. I was actually chatting and talking to the interviewees while picking and packing orders. This way, no one could be under any illusions as to what the job was all about. It also helped me get some of the shipping done a bit quicker because the good candidates got stuck in and helped out during their interview. It was an effective interview process and it helped me find an exceptional employee in Kathy.

My Little Wrapper continues to thrive, and the market for personalised chocolate is showing no signs of being hampered or hindered by the economic downturn. In fact, the opposite is true. People like their chocolate and the personalisation that we've got is a great little product. Business is booming.

As always, we've spawned a number of copycats. There are other people that are trying to get in on our market, and that's understandable and to be expected. I've learnt from the past that when you uncover a new market and are successful, other people are going to come in there and try and copy your business model. But we do what we do very well. We more than hold our own, and, of course, we were first – and that counts for a lot.

CHAPTER 10
GETTING THE BEST OUT OF PEOPLE

When I started N5, I was very ambitious. While I wasn't quite sure what we were going to end up doing, I knew I wanted to build a big business. If you set up a business on your own, at some point you have to make a decision. You can either get stuck in and do all the work yourself – thereby limiting your income – or you can hire some employees and seek to grow with other people's help. I was definitely in that latter camp. I wanted to grow.

There have always been a lot of opportunities around that I wanted to exploit, as you've repeatedly seen throughout this book. I wanted to make the business bigger and so, from the early days of N5, I built a team.

I've had some great people on my staff – individuals like Audrey, who I employed to do the telephone selling for me, right up to more recent times with the hiring of Kathy for My Little Wrapper. I've been fortunate enough to have some really great employees on my team – people who are pretty much worth their weight in gold. They are out there.

Give Me Attitude Every Time

What I'm pulling together in this chapter is my learning and observations on all aspects of hiring, managing, leading, and dealing with staff. I've learned a heck of a lot about it from my very direct, first-hand experience over the last eight years, allied, of course, to my experience before that in Barclays, CPP and the other organisations.

One thing I did very consciously within N5 was to hire for attitude, not experience. I was very keen in the beginning that my business would be an energetic, passionate place to work; that we would move fast, deliver fast and make things happen. I guess in many ways what I was articulating is almost a manifestation of my own personality, and I wanted the business to reflect that. It was my business, after all.

Over time, though, I learned that you do need balance!

My policy of hiring for attitude was a good one, and it helped us make the most of those heady days of hyper-growth from 2005–2007. As the business developed, and we got beyond 30 employees, I recognised that I did need to hire some people that knew 'the how'. In other words they had experience of previously doing whatever it was I was asking them to do. You see, I had been all about bringing on smart, bright, hungry, people with great attitude who could learn – which is great – but if everyone is having to learn everything… well, that's not so good! So, in more recent years, I've hired people that brought experience and expertise into my business. They've still got a great attitude, mind you!

For the right people, working within my business is the best job in the world. That's not me being arrogant or big-headed (as if!), it's true. They have a level of responsibility, an opportunity to shape things, create things and do things that really isn't available in most organisations.

Botty's Rule No. 20
Bite-sized goals are good.

I keep my team focused on the near-future – typically the next three months. Their goals are predominantly short-term and 'bite-size'. This makes it easier (for them and me) to stay focused and single-minded on what needs doing.

There's still only a tiny proportion of business owners who write down their goals. Those of us that do tend to achieve, or more often, overachieve, what we wrote down. Whereas, the people that never write anything down rarely achieve super-success.

I prefer to work with bite-sized goals. What I mean by that are things that we can get done in one, two or three months, something that is almost tangible in terms of how close it is. I've never been one for big strategic planning, three-year business plans, and huge long-term goals. In my experience, life's never been like that, so I work in a much tighter time frame. But I'm very specific, and I do write my goals down. I know that most people don't do this and I also know that most people don't get quite as much done as we do. There is a definite connection.

Underpinning all of this is a level of clarity as to what you want to achieve. Again, I don't think this needs to be cerebrally taxing; you just need to be specific about what you want to implement and then make it happen. Keeping it simple is definitely de rigueur here.

Culture and Vibe

I get regular feedback from people that visit our headquarters in Solihull for the first time; they always comment on the vibe in our business. That's something I'm proud of, but it's also something that we work specifically to create. The atmosphere in our offices is not an accident. It didn't happen by chance. There is clear strategic direction within the business. If you were to talk to any of my staff and ask them where the business was going, what matters most and what the focus is on, you would get a very common and consistent set of answers. Having that level of clarity right throughout the organisation is, I believe, crucial for success. It's an important part of leadership – people work better when they understand where the company is going and what their role in that is.

The right people enjoy working with me. They feed off my ideas, my vision and my energy, so I need to keep doses of that flowing through the organisation. But some staff have come into our organisation and found it to be just the most horrible place to work. It's not for everyone. If you're looking for a nice, steady job where things don't change much, where there are clearly written down processes for everything that you need to do, where everything is planned out many months in advance, where nothing much new ever happens, then N5 is not for you. We're very different to that.

The culture is another thing that we put quite a bit of thought and effort into. Our offices are decorated differently than most offices. We have brightly coloured, striped walls. While not a big thing (and by the way, it doesn't cost any more money to paint the walls striped in six different colours than it does to paint them white or cream), it does bring a different feel to the place.

We have table football tables and Friday afternoon beers. By no means is it a youth club environment, but it's a place that people like to be. People feel very comfortable. The dress code is very relaxed, and all this 'physicality' of culture helps with clarity of purpose and direction. Incidentally, we have virtually no work days lost due to sickness. It's almost unheard of for someone to not come in (and that doesn't happen by accident – it's a direct result of the vibe going on in the workplace) *and* we get a heck of a lot done. I believe my team is at least 50% more efficient at getting stuff done than most organisations. This stuff works. We've got an effective set-up, and I'm certainly very fortunate that the vast majority of my staff do care a great deal about this business. (But, again, it didn't happen by accident!)

More Right than Wrong

There are 34 members of my team at the time of writing, plus a handful of key outsourced partners, and they are all very committed to the success of the business and to their role within it. That leads to good things for our customers and, indeed, for the business itself. So, how do you find great staff that behave like that, think like that and have emotionally bought into what you're doing? After all, good staff are hard to find, aren't they?

Well, what I've come to realise over the years is that all you can really hope for when it comes to hiring staff is to get it more right than you get wrong. I don't believe that there is any foolproof way to guarantee that someone you're taking on board is going to be a blow-away success. There are things you can do to help ensure it's not the opposite of that, but you can never be certain that they're going to be absolutely fantastic until they've been in the workplace doing the job for some time.

The biggest mistakes I've made in hiring have been with people that I know. For instance, I had a personal assistant named Julie, the relation of a friend of mine. He suggested that she'd be great as my PA. So I met with her; she seemed a nice lady (I mean, what was I thinking! What sort of criteria was that?), so I employed her. At the end of the first week she came in to see me in my office. She shut the door and said, 'Nigel, you need to change.'

That was an absurd thing for her to say. Perhaps had I been quick enough, my response to her should have been, 'Yeah, you're right, I need to change my PA.'

That is actually what happened quickly thereafter, but I dragged it out over a few weeks. Never forget who is working for whom.

So now I've got this unwritten rule – I'm not going to fix myself. At 45 years of age, I'm comfortable in my own skin and I'm not going to change or adapt to suit my employees. That's not going to happen; it's my business not theirs, and they work for me – not the other way round. So I need to find people that are comfortable with my business, my personality, our culture and me.

I've been ripped off twice by employees who have set up in competition with me while they were still working for me. Now, apart from being really stupid (did they really think I wouldn't find out?), this is just a massively unethical thing to do but they did it anyway. Don't misunderstand me here – I'm all in favour of competition. But at least have the balls to be open about it, and don't take a pay cheque from someone that you are implicitly trying to put out of business (ultimately that's what competition boils down to) and don't schmooze with colleagues who you are secretly trying to make unemployed and don't steal information and databases. Bastards.

They didn't get to me, really!

In both cases, their businesses failed spectacularly. I think business is a bit like top-class sport in that respect. When you watch it on TV or up close, it always looks so easy and straightforward. But when you try and play golf like Lee Westwood, or kick a football like David Beckham, or play tennis like Rafael Nadal, you can't – because it's hard. There's lots going on inside their brains and body that are invisible and they've spent years to learn and perfect. It's just like that in business – but my two erstwhile colleagues weren't smart enough to see it. They thought it was easy to do what we do. They thought there was nothing to it and that they could easily copy it and enjoy the same success. They were wrong ... on all accounts.

It's easy in those situations to get rid of people. They were both fired within an hour of my finding out what they'd been up to. They were escorted off the premises, and I made sure everyone in the team knew what they'd been up to. I don't have any issues about sacking someone when they're behaving like that. When their moral code is so flawed, it's easy, frankly.

23 Points on her Licence

We hired a very bright young lady one time to fulfil a field sales role. She was going to be out and about selling, and we got a company car sorted for her. It looked like she was going to be a great fit for the job. She had a good track record, her references checked out, she was a good cultural fit and hopes were high. It was only on her first morning when Brenda asked her for a copy of her driving licence and some questions for the car insurance form that she told us about her seven driving convictions. Seven. She had 23 points. Bear in mind that she was only 23 years of age (that's a point for every year of her age!) and that none these were for minor offences. She'd been done twice for drunk driving, once for leaving the scene of an accident, once for driving without due care and attention and once for reckless driving. Even if she'd still had a licence, she would have been uninsurable, but she was still banned, so she couldn't fulfil her job because she couldn't drive.

Why she didn't tell us earlier in the recruitment process, I have no idea. So, she was only in our offices for about three hours while this was all sorted out. Of course, she had to leave. We sacked her before lunch on her first day and she holds the record for shortest time ever in the employ of N5, but that wasn't the last we heard of her.

Two weeks later the cheeky lady sued us because she said she'd slipped and fallen on a staff room floor. This was a total fabrication, and we were able to deal with it fairly easily, but it gives you a further insight into her character. I reckon we had a lucky escape with that one!

What was also interesting, by the way, was that the recruitment agency through which we found her refused to credit or replace her. They wouldn't accept any responsibility and they kept their £3,500 fee, which is a really bad way to carry on in business. As a result, we stopped using them, and I made a point of telling everyone I knew in and around Solihull about how they treated us. They ceased trading last year. What goes around comes around.

We've had a catalogue of bad experiences with hiring people, as well as lots of good ones. I hired a PA once who thought she actually ran the company rather than being the PA to the guy that ran the company. That got completely out of hand, and she had to go.

BA's In-Flight Magazine Changed our Business for Ever!

I made the decision to hire my first salesperson when I was on an airplane flying to America. I was reading the BA in-flight magazine, and there was an advertorial feature about the late John Harvey Jones. He was recommending a company called Meta-Morphose. They were a recruitment company that only placed graduates or graduate-calibre people that had a high propensity to be successful in sales. They not only placed these people, but they guaranteed if they left you within a year, they would replace them at no charge. They also trained and developed them, which was exactly the service I was looking for.

As soon as I got off the plane in America, I rang them up and managed to get some work underway while I was in the States. When I came back home five days later, some interviews had been set up, and I met five great candidates. I was only looking to hire one person but two of the candidates were really excellent, and I couldn't decide which one to take on. I went home that night and talked with Sue about my dilemma. Finding really good people is hard. They're increasingly rare, and the conclusion Sue and I came to was that we should take them both – which I did, and Cat and Thom are still with us today. They are both star members of the N5 team.

Over the past four years, pretty much all of my salespeople have been hired through Meta-Morphose. It's a great service. Although it's a lot more expensive than most recruitment companies, the value that they provide more than justifies the cost. Business owners often confuse cost with value, or else don't understand that there's a difference. There is – a huge difference – and value matters much more.

Short-Term Pain or Long-Term Pain

If you're going to grow a super-successful business, then you are going to have to hire and fire staff. I'm always genuinely surprised about business owners' eagerness to do one and reluctance to do the other. What I've learnt is that people tend to hire fast and fire slow. They need someone and therefore they snatch up the first person that comes along. Then, when problems start to emerge, entrepreneurs are very reluctant to deal with it. They avoid conflict. Big mistake.

I've found the opposite way is the right way to go. I would actively encourage business owners to hire slow. Take your time and make sure you're finding the right person. But if you get it wrong, then fire fast because, in your business, you can either have long-term pain or short-term pain.

I've tried both and I can tell you without any shadow of a doubt, short-term pain is better. Having said that, I've hardly ever been as quick to get rid of people as I should have been, but I'm not bad at it, and there are a few things I've learnt along the way. Some of these lessons have been really painful, including one that I still count as my single biggest mistake in business, which I'll tell you about in a moment.

First of all, though, when I look back, I can see that the attitude is always wrong in the staff that have left. If I trace it back, there were signs before anything material started to appear or anything tangible like poor performance.

When you are telling someone that they're leaving your organisation, whether you are going down the disciplinary route of dismissing them for poor performance or the redundancy route – and I've done both– what I have learnt is that all they hear in that meeting is the fact that they are leaving and nothing else you say gets heard.

Therefore, there's no point really in saying it. It's much better to have everything written down in a letter, tell them they're leaving, give them the letter and then get them off the premises; that certainly has been our process. You definitely need a good lawyer. If you do things properly and follow the right processes, then you won't have any problems. We have never, ever been involved in a single tribunal. This is because we did everything right. We had the right contracts, and we followed the right processes. We're also studiously fair. But it's also because I've been prepared to write the cheque and move on.

In a couple of instances in particular, I have effectively dismissed someone and given them a cheque to go. It was the best way because the issue gets dealt with. The pain is short, both from a time and a financial perspective. It's dealt with. I can move on with developing and building the business, and they can move on with their lives. The distraction within the business lasts only a few hours, and then we're back on track and running again. That has been an important lesson for me. It's business, not personal, and everything has a price.

Which brings me to my single worst decision ever in business. Incidentally, the best book I've read about managing people is by the great Dan Kennedy. It's called *No BS Ruthless Management of People & Profits*. It's very forthright but absolutely on the money. You should buy a copy and study it (but don't let your staff see it!).

A £250,000 Mistake

I hired one person who cost me over a quarter of a million pounds in just 15 months. That doesn't include their salary and all the time and energy and angst. That was over £250,000 cash out the door. Very painful indeed.

When I analyse this, I realise my first mistake was that I hired too quickly. This guy was a friend of a friend, and I never asked for his references. I believed everything he told me and I gave him responsibility for my marketing, which was a really stupid thing to do. Everything we've achieved has been on the back of effective marketing – which I had driven. Why, therefore, would I want to suddenly relinquish that to someone who, in truth, I knew very little about and who had done nothing with me to suggest that he was capable? What was I thinking? (Ain't hindsight a wonderful thing.)

My (flawed) logic said that by handing marketing over to him I would be able to do other things and create new businesses and opportunities, so I stepped away, developed other businesses and projects and took my eye completely off the marketing ball. He asked for responsibility; I gave it to him.

He started to apply big, corporate marketing techniques to what is not a big, corporate business. He started placing brand adverts in magazines and newspapers, costing a lot of money. (Previously, we had used direct-response ads, which at least makes the ad accountable and we can track responses.)

It was completely ridiculous. There was no tracking on our marketing, no accountability and, crucially, hardly any bloody sales! And it was all my fault.

He spent over £200,000 on ads that didn't work but it all came to a head over a particular issue with regard to an exhibition, and our access to the database of visitors to the exhibition. When I invoked the disciplinary process, he lodged seven separate grievances against me and four against his colleagues. He wrote a letter, setting out his grievances, and in the same envelope was another letter saying, 'If you drop the disciplinary, pay me this chunk of money, I'll leave and drop the grievance ...'

He was gone within 30 minutes.

Write the cheque and move on; it's always the best way.

Setting the Standards

In 2006, as we started to grow and our head count started to get into double figures, I sat and wrote down what I wanted my company to be like. I came up with a set of rules for working at N5.

The rules set out very clearly my expectations of people in the company. It's a really useful thing to have, both at interview stage so that people see the sort of business we are ('This is what our expectations will be of you and of you working around here …') and to keep things on track when people occasionally forget! Our 'Rules' appear on a big A1 poster on every floor in our offices so everyone can see them every single day.

By the way, I'm not saying that they're right for your business, but they're right for us. You should come up with your own rules, but take a look at ours as a starting point:

N5's Golden Rules

We want everyone that works at N5 to feel that they are part of a successful team, and that they are respected, appreciated and rewarded for the good work they do. Above all, we want people to enjoy working at N5; these standards help us all to know what is expected of us.

Rule #1: We Work a Fair and Full Day This means that time at work is spent productively! Personal stuff needs to be kept to a minimum; this includes taking personal calls, sending texts, checking Facebook or chatting on Twitter or MSN ...

Rule #2: We're a Team We're all in this together. Being a team means that it is never 'not my job'.

Rule #3: We're Proud of our Work Because we take pride in the work we do, we do it as it is intended to be done. No short cuts, omissions, bodge-jobs or work-arounds! We will support every employee who delivers a fair, just, full day of compliant work by not saddling them with the slack of any bad employees.

Rule #4 We Respect our Franchisees Our franchisees are our customers – and we will treat them as such. They pay our wages and are the reason for our existence. We always seek to understand them, to see things from their point of view and we never slag them off.

Rule #5: We Keep our Promises When we say we'll do something or we'll get back to someone, we do it. We don't let people down – colleagues, customers or suppliers.

Rule #6: We're Positive It's not okay to say negative things about the company or any of our customers or staff. We won't tolerate – at all – anything or anyone that contributes negative word-of-mouth.

Rule #7: We Don't Do Things Slowly We do them quickly or not at all. This means that there'll always be lots going on – and things will change as we adapt and spot new opportunities. It's never been calm around here, and as long as we're successful, it never will be!

Rule #8: We're in Business to Make Profit
We're not here for fun. Creating profit is fundamental to any successful company and the people we value most are the ones who contribute most to profit. It's not

enough to be busy; as teams and as individuals, we need to ask ourselves, 'What are we busy doing?' If you're not focusing on profit, you're doing something wrong ... It's okay for anybody to question anybody else, at any time, about what they're doing and how it contributes to profit.

Rule #9: We Finish Stuff Our key measures of success and performance will be based around what you got done, not what you are doing. We don't like activity masquerading as accomplishment – you need to focus on getting things done. Not 'doing' or 'in the pipeline', but properly done. Finished. Crossed off. Achieved.

Rule #10: We Recognise and Reward Good Thinking We can all find better, more efficient ways to work – and we've all got a responsibility to speak up and share ideas.

Rule #11: We Think Before We Act Making an honest mistake when you've thought something through and did things for the right reasons is fine. In fact, it's encouraged. However, doing something dumb because you didn't think is unforgivable.

Rule #12: We Don't Clock-Watch Working at N5 means putting in some extra hours – this isn't 'face-time' – we do it because we enjoy working here, and we believe in what we're doing.

Rule #13: We Work Hard, Play Hard and Eat Lunch At lunch, we get out of the office. Eating at our desks is an exception. We all need breaks to work effectively.

Rule #14: We Keep our Workplace Tidy Everything should have a home – we don't let stuff congregate by the sides of desks, in corridors, in reception or under the stairs.

To be honest about it, I do expect more from my staff than most businesses do. Part of the reason for that is because I get a lot more *from* my staff. They deliver. My team is brilliant, and I'm very very fortunate to work with such good people. Thanks, guys.

Having hired people, you've got to manage them properly. I learnt a lot about management from a book by Marcus Buckingham called *First, Break all the Rules*. I first discovered this when I was working at Barclays. It helped to shape some of my philosophies and approaches back in those days, but it's particularly relevant when you're running your own business. One of the things that Buckingham discusses in his book, and I've certainly found it to be true, is that in day-to-day situations in business, the manager, boss or leader naturally finds his time drawn to dealing with the poorest performers.

How Do You Manage?

We are always sucked in, trying to fix the issues that we've got with the people who are performing least well. Don't believe me? Try this short exercise:

- Draw three columns.
- In the left-hand column, list all the staff that work for you in order of their effectiveness/productivity. How good they are at the job, how much you rely and depend on them, the value of the contribution they provide to your business. So, you write the name of your most productive, most valuable employee at the top of that column and the least valuable/least productive at the bottom of that column.
- Leave the middle column blank and in the right-hand column, list your staff based on the amount of time you

spend with them – with the name of the person you spend most time with at the top and the person you spend least time with at the bottom.

- Next, connect the names using the space in the middle column. So draw a line from Peter's name in the left column to Peter's name in the right column.

What you'll typically find is that the two lists are almost completely opposite. The people at the bottom of one list are at the top of the other. It certainly used to be the case for me. If you find that's the case for you, then you're sabotaging your business – in a major way.

In his book, Buckingham argues the case that this is a very dumb position to be in. He outlines very clearly that if you want to move your business and your team forward, then what you need to do is spend most of your time with your top performers. Your business will accelerate away. They will take you further, and faster, than you'll ever get by trying to make your poor performers catch up.

That is something that I've tried very hard to work on. I do avoid spending time with my poorest performers. I enjoy spending time with my top performers. We spark off each other. We inspire each other, and my business is better because of that.

During 2007, as part of Andy Hurst's arrival in the company, I embarked on a very deliberate policy to ensure I was removing dependency on any one person. My plan was to ensure that the business was not dependent on any single individual – for anything – so that if anybody resigned or left the organisation for any reason, it wouldn't be a crisis. At least one other person would be able to do their job.

This is a very important thing for every business to do, and I wish I'd done it sooner. I had been lucky in that I was

Botty's Rule No. 21
You've got to stop the sabotage ...

This applies particularly if you employ staff – although not exclusively so. What I mean by sabotage is things happening in your business that you don't want to happen and that are diminishing either your level of sales or your level of customer service. Let me give you an example to make my point.

I was in a very nice restaurant for Sunday lunch a few weeks ago. It's part of a small national chain. I noticed that when the waiters were bringing the bill out to the other tables, the bills were being presented on top of a nice blue postcard. I also noticed that no one was filling in the postcard. I was intrigued to see what was on it. When we finished our meal, the waiter brought the bill on a little silver tray sat on top of a nice blue postcard. It was all wonderfully branded, and it was a straightforward play for them to capture contact details and build their database. A big tick.

What had happened here is that the marketing manager at head office decided that they ought to try and build a database and collect contact information, which is clearly the right thing to do. He or she had commissioned a designer, and they'd done a good job designing a very nice postcard that was functional and looked appropriate. Then all the restaurant managers had been briefed and they, in turn, had to brief their staff about the new process for handing out the bills and what to do with the cards, etc. In short, a lot of effort had gone into getting that postcard onto my table, and everyone

else's table in that restaurant that day – yet no one was filling them in. Why not?

There were two reasons. Firstly, there was no pen. This is the classic ship being sunk but for a ha'poth of tar. The second reason was that none of the staff ever mentioned the postcard or made a request for it to be filled in. If they had just said, 'Here's your bill, sir. While I go and get the credit card machine, if you'd just fill your details in on this postcard, we'll be able to keep you in touch about a series of wine-tasting and food events and also some special offers. We want to make sure you don't miss out on anything in the months ahead.' If they'd have done that and handed you a pen at the same time, they would have got most people to fill those cards in. As it was, they got hardly anyone. Sabotage.

What's happening in your business today, this week, that's sabotaging your results? If you want to be super-successful, you've got to find it and stop it.

never really caught out with any big issues, but I could have been. Now every task, every process, everything in the business is understood and known about and can be done by at least two people. There are two reasons for that – firstly, it gives us operational resilience, which is smart. Secondly, it ensures that no one is indispensable.

'How Was your Weekend?'

Another element with managing people is that you have to find time to just walk around the place; you've got to keep your eye on what's going on. When My Little Wrapper went a bit tits-up, and I had to fix it, the reason it got to the state it did was because I hadn't been paying enough attention to it. I got sucked into other things.

I know pretty much everything that goes on in my business. I could fulfil any role tomorrow (with the exception of the technical developers) and that's a good place to be because it helps me ensure that everything is pretty much in order and under control. When you are walking around, of course, you do have to pay attention to what people say and listen appropriately; you can't just do this by diary.

I'm reminded of a little story here from very early in my career. I was working at Barclays at the Leeds University branch. The manager of that branch, my boss, was a very friendly man named Geoff Sharpe. Geoff didn't like to walk around. His office was on the upper floor and all the staff worked downstairs. Geoff used to come downstairs on Monday morning at 9.30. It was the only time in the week we would ever see him downstairs and he would do his little 'management by walking around'. He would start off saying, 'How was your weekend?' People would say, 'Oh yes, very

good, thank you, Mr Sharpe.' And he'd reply, 'Oh good, good.'
And he'd move on to the next person without really listening
to what people were saying.

We proved it to him one morning. My colleague Neil
Gascoigne and I planned a stitch-up. Mr Sharpe came round
as usual, and when he got to Neil, he asked his usual question,
'How was your weekend?'

Neil replied, with a completely straight face, 'Oh not
good, thanks. My mother died.'

'Oh good, good,' said Geoff, and off he went. He'd not
heard a word that had been said. I was bent double on the
floor. It was so funny, it hurt.

Of course, once you have a team of staff you have to allow
and enable them to do their jobs. As I started to grow my business, my staff were just assistants to me. The only work they
did was what I asked them to do. Everything came through
me. I signed off on everything. I triggered every piece of work.
I don't think this is uncommon among entrepreneurs – but it
is a big problem.

As well as being hugely stressful to me, ultimately it's also
unfulfilling for them, especially if they're high-calibre people.
It also wasn't very effective for the business because we were
still constrained by what I could do mentally and physically,
and that's not a good place to be.

Andy Hurst's arrival helped me a lot with this. We've got
a proper management structure now. People have clear
responsibilities, goals and objectives. It's very important when
your business grows that you have to let go at the right point.
One of our rules, as you've seen, is that your mistakes are
okay as long as things are thought through. I've kind of got
used to that now – I know that we will make the occasional
cock-up, but it's not the end of the world, providing people

are learning as a result. Every now and again, stupid things happen in any business, and I have to remind myself of this.

I look at this way – we're getting 600% more done than we could ever achieve if everything was having to come through me. If 5% of the 600% is done wrong, or not quite right, then we're still so far ahead of where we would be. Make sense?

Getting Stuff Done

I often get asked by people how we get so much done in our company. There are three answers to this.

The first one is deadlines.

The second one is deadlines.

And the third one is deadlines. (Remember Botty's Rule No. 5.)

Everything we do is driven by deadlines and this has been key to us making such rapid progress on so many fronts.

We're also very focused, which is another key to us getting a lot done. We do a lot of stuff, but it's pretty well focused on the same set of strategic goals. I think far too many companies lose focus when they try to do too much, and that's certainly something we've been guilty of in the past. As I've said on page 144, one of the curses of being an entrepreneur is that we are attracted by bright, shiny objects. We like new things, and that can be dangerous because sometimes what we need most is to knuckle down, follow through and deliver properly on the project we already started. A lot of people just start another one alongside it.

Here's an interesting analogy for you. Think about your business as being like the Grand National. You wouldn't swap horses in the middle of the race. If you're a jockey on a horse, you are in the moment. You are focused on the horse that you're riding. You want to get to the winning post, and if you don't get there first, you want to at least come in second or third. What a jockey does not do at any point during the race is even think about climbing onto another horse.

Yet entrepreneurs in a similar situation often do exactly that.

By the way, don't come back at me and tell me there are people in the circus that can ride two horses at once. I know that's true, but they are rare, they're highly skilled, and they never win horse races! This is what I tried to do with Quickie, and it just didn't work.

Jockeys only ride one horse at any one time, and in that respect, I try and keep my people focused on single projects with tight deadlines, so they're making progress, getting things delivered and then they're on to the next one. Just like a jockey. Driving it through, getting things done and finished is important. In that respect, having clarity of responsibilities so people know exactly what they've got to do is essential.

Rewarding Staff

I've been asked many times if and how I reward my staff. Most of them have the opportunity to earn bonuses; we have different bonus schemes, depending on what their roles are.

In addition, key members of my management team, the people at the core of my business that I depend on the most, have options on some shares in the company. This means that if, at some point in the future, the business is sold, then they will be able to participate in the proceeds of that sale. I think that's an entirely fair and equitable thing to do.

There is a contrary argument that the entrepreneur and publisher Felix Dennis articulates, which is never, ever give them a share of the rock, but I disagree with him on this. I think done at the right level, it's the right thing to do. I know that for some of them, their share options are the most important part of their package with N5. There's evidence to suggest that it definitely helps in terms of their commitment, their dedication and their enthusiasm because they've got that little share of the rock, so I am an advocate and a fan of modest share options for key members of staff.

Our bonus schemes are based on performance. My sales guys can earn a bonus monthly, based on revenue that they bring in. Other staff earn bonuses for on-time delivery of projects and company performance over the year.

It's often the little things that make the biggest difference. When my tech team delivered our '14 Days of Love' campaign (more of which later) in less than four weeks, I sent them down to Villa Park to watch Man United play Aston Villa. Cost me less than £300 in total, but they had a great night. It was impromptu, immediate and for three of them the first time they'd been to a Premiership game. It had a great impact – and was very cost-effective.

One of my top team members had a birthday last week. On Saturday morning, she received a huge bouquet of flowers from Sue and me, which we had delivered to her home. We don't do that for everyone on their birthday, but she's done some amazing work for us in recent months, so we decided that was the right thing to do. Cost me £80, but she was over the moon. She's telling everyone about her great job and amazing boss. It was worth every penny and definitely got more 'bang-for-buck' than slipping £80 into her pay packet.

My staff know that if they need time off in a crisis that I'll support them. It's all about give and take. All my good team members regularly work extra hours, so when something happens in their life that means they need a bit of time off I'll always accommodate them. It's just smart business. Take some time and sort it out – then come back focused and energised is my mantra there.

I'm writing this chapter in the middle of the World Cup. I met a guy yesterday who has 40 staff. He's insisting that those that want to watch the England game against Slovenia come in at 7 a.m. tomorrow so that they can finish at 3 p.m. to watch it – and they have to watch it off the premises. He's bonkers.

At N5, my team will be stopping work at 2.45 p.m. We're all convening in our training suite, and we're having a World Cup party. We'll stick the phones on voicemail, I'll supply some beer and nibbles and we'll have a great time. It will do far more for morale and productivity than forcing people to come in early.

When it comes to building a crack team and motivating your staff, you have to look at the wider picture. Money is not everybody's biggest motivator. Some of my guys are really keen on personal development. There are conferences or courses that they'd like to go on, so we use that as a reward mechanism. It's all quite informal but what's unwritten between us is that you do a great job and I'll give you time off to go to those events. I'll even fund them as well, if they're relevant to the business. People love this.

There are a couple of big events that I go to every year in America. For the last three years now, I take two members of my team with me. We don't fly economy – and it ain't cheap – but the value I get from them being exposed to new thinking and being able to focus with them 100% on our business for 18 hours a day for five days is worth a fortune. In fact, on our last trip I concluded that just the eight-hour flight to Dallas was worth the trip on its own – because we got so much thinking and planning done. It would never have happened if we'd stayed in the office.

We've been fortunate to be nominated for several major awards over the years, including some of the most prestigious awards available to British businesses. Taking half a dozen of my staff with me to the awards presentations was hugely motivating for them. We'd get chauffeur driven to London, meet lots of celebs and, on a few occasions, actually win the award. Those nights had a big impact on all the staff.

Rewarding your staff comes in many different guises. It's about the environment, the work and the leadership just as much as the money. There are many ways that you can reward and recognise contribution – you just have to be alert for the opportunities and recognise that one size definitely doesn't fit all.

CHAPTER 11
THEBESTOF ROLLS ON ...

While other parts of the business have been developing and some, like *Raring2Go!*, have been sold, thebestof has continued to grow. It's remained, since its launch, the biggest single part of my business. As I'm writing this in the summer of 2010, we have over 60,000 UK businesses that are paid up members of thebestof.

Most of those are spread across 144 core business types – for example, accountants, printers, plumbers, hairdressers and bouncy castle hire companies, to name just a few. They are the sorts of businesses that local people need on a regular basis all around the country, and they are at the heart of all our local business communities.

We have just over 400 franchise areas in operation, but only about 250 franchisees. That's because we have what I believe is the highest proportion of multiple franchise owners of any franchise in the UK. No one can come on board and buy multiple areas at the beginning. They have to start with a single area, get that up and running and build success. Once they've achieved that, if they want to expand their business into other areas then we allow them to do that, providing they meet all the relevant criteria.

It's quite a testament to the success of thebestof and its business model that we have so many franchisees that have acquired second and third and, in a few cases, four additional franchise areas. We have several of our franchisees now earning six-figure sums, and the business has really flourished and grown, even during the economic downturn. When you analyse it, it's not hard to see why.

Let's face it, if you were a local business owner in the period from the end of the Second World War up to the turn of the millennium, then the way you marketed your business was pretty consistent throughout all that time. You took out the biggest ad you could afford in the Yellow Pages. You also relied on word-of-mouth and if you were really flash (or ambitious), you took an ad in the local newspaper. There wasn't much else, but there didn't need to be. That was how you marketed your business, and it worked.

That's all been thrown on its head in the past few years. Most people don't use the printed Yellow Pages books at all any more, and they won't even be printed within 10 years. Local newspapers have seen their advertising revenues plummet in recent times as readership numbers fall.

The Internet has caused a seismic shift in the way local businesses can market themselves, and thebestof has been really well positioned to exploit that shift and provide our customers with much better marketing value, for much less cost, than they were ever getting before from a single advertising media.

thebestof is a business with a website – NOT a website business, don't forget. Much of what we do happens offline and the wide variety of ways in which we champion and promote our member businesses make for a very compelling proposition, which is why it's grown so fast and has such a solid customer base.

Botty's Rule No. 22
The Power of Testimonials.

What other people say about you carries about 500 times as much weight as what you say about yourself – so use testimonials in your marketing.

This is a very self-explanatory rule. Most people will instinctively recognise and agree with it. Yet, if that is the case, why do so few business owners incorporate testimonials and case studies into their marketing? Don't believe me? Take a look around. It's really quite unusual to find businesses utilising testimonials.

On thebestof, we were the first website in the UK to allow people to leave reviews and testimonials of local businesses. We know that our member businesses that have dozens of testimonials get lots more enquiries and phone calls than those that have only one or two.

Many of our tradespeople use our postcards and online mechanisms to collect testimonials from their customers. On the bottom of all their stationery and quotes they say, 'Find out what our customers say about us by visiting ...' (they insert their bestof web page address). These smart people recognise the power of testimonials and endorsements and are using them appropriately. If you aspire to super-success, you need to do the same.

Establishing trust and confidence with your potential customers is one of the biggest hurdles any business owner has to overcome. Real, authentic specific testimonials from real, authentic customers (ideally with a full name and a photograph!) can make a huge difference to your conversion rate.

Our Single Most Powerful Sales Tool ...

Interestingly, we have long advocated that our business members get their customers to write about how good they are and what it is that makes them good but we'd never acted on this advice ourselves ... until very recently. Just before Christmas 2009, I asked a couple of my staff to ring up businesses in each of our 144 core categories, and ask them a single question: 'How are you getting on with thebestof?'

I asked them to write down everything that they said.

The responses we received were amazing, and we turned them into a very large book that has become the single most powerful sales tool that we've got. All we ask businesses to do, if they're interested in coming on board with thebestof, is to read through the book, so that they get a feel for what our existing customers say about us. There are over 400 comments in there from business owners around the country, and they are all ordered by business type/category. The comments are all substantive, with people explaining how and why thebestof is working so well for them. Two things strike you as you read the book. The first is, 'Crikey, there are a lot of businesses doing very well with this' because there are such a lot of comments in there.

The second thing is, 'Gosh there's a lot to this, thebestof does a lot of things.' This is because each business talks about how one (or more!) element of our proposition is working for them. Some talk about how they get lots of new customers from our door drops. Other businesses will talk about how our networking meetings are key for them getting new business. Some will talk about the 'Mix and match', and how it's our franchisees that plug them together and introduce them personally to new customers. Others might mention our website. A lot of tradespeople explain in the book how it's the testimonials that we've helped them collect, and which are available for everyone to see on the website, that are helping them to get business – even when they're not the cheapest quote.

The whole breadth of our proposition comes through really powerfully in this book of testimonials. In many ways, it was a big mistake not to have pulled this together much earlier, but now that we do have it, as I said, it's the single best sales tool we've got.

Off to Wembley

One Tuesday afternoon, out of the blue, I got a call from the *Sunday Times* Tech Track team. They'd apparently been tracking our growth and they explained that they thought we were eligible for placing in the *Sunday Times*/Microsoft Tech Track 100 – a list of the 100 fastest growing technology-based businesses in the UK.

It all sounded very exciting, until they told me that we'd have to allow a team from Price Waterhouse Coopers to crawl over our business to verify whether or not we should be included.

The accountants came and went and a few weeks later I hurried to the newsagent very early on Sunday morning to see where we had been placed (they really don't tell you until it's published). We were No. 3! The third-fastest growing tech-based company in the country. This was really exciting.

The following day, I received a very smart invitation to dinner at Wembley stadium. We were only allowed two places, so Sue and I made a night of it. All the great and the good from British business were there, and we were presented with our third-place award. Good times.

'People' People …

Now, while we have a lot of franchisees that are doing very well with thebestof, not everybody is a soaring success. We lose franchisees occasionally. Several have died. Three have emigrated. Some have health problems, either their own that of a close family member. Some have got divorced or other life-changing things have happened, but when a franchisee does leave us, in almost all cases, it's created a great opportunity.

In one instance, we had a franchisee in Scotland that had run the business for over two years. During the last nine months that she was with us, she became quite downcast. She convinced herself that thebestof wouldn't work in her area, she felt that businesses weren't looking for what we did and that the local people didn't want to use thebestof in the way that they were in other parts of the country.

She really was talking herself out of business, and it became a self-fulfilling prophecy. We needed to exit her – quickly. We managed to find a new franchisee to take on that area. When this new franchisee inherited it, they took on a business that was doing about £2,000 a month turnover, which is very small for a business like thebestof, particularly one that's been established for a couple of years. Within six months, they had built a five-figure monthly turnover. It was the same business with the same proposition in the same town, all that was different was the people running it. Instead of no customers, they now have a waiting list of customers wanting to join. My point here is that the biggest single dependency that determines the success of thebestof in any particular area is the person running it – which is true in virtu-ally any business, of course. It's just that in a franchise like ours, the impact is much more visible.

A similar thing happened down in Cheltenham where Simon Bullingham took over a business that had been, at best, struggling to get by. Simon has completely transformed thebestof in Cheltenham into a very big business with a large customer base and huge profile. He's also pioneered many of the new elements of our proposition – our Handy Blue Book, for instance and our use of billboards and buses (to promote not only our own brand but also all our customers), not to mention the first-ever thebestof shop, were all conceived of and trialled in Cheltenham.

As a result of all our learning, we're much fussier now about whom we allow to run a franchise. Among other things, we're looking for people that are entrepreneurial. thebestof is a business that can't be defined precisely in a manual from Solihull. You need to be sufficiently aware, alert and tuned in to spot opportunities on your patch. A guy named Alex Murray recently took over thebestof in Walsall. Walsall is another franchise area that had just kind of plodded along for two or three years before he came in and bought the franchise. He has really, metaphorically speaking, set Walsall on fire with what he's done there to build the profile, the brand and build strategic partnerships with key organisations in the town. He's made of a very big impact in just a few months because of his entrepreneurial flair.

We want franchisees that are ambitious. If people are looking to run a business that will pay them £3,000–4,000 per month income, than I'd rather they went somewhere else because there are loads of franchises in the UK that can deliver that. We are seeking franchisees that want something bigger than that; so ambition is an important element in our criteria.

I'll be frank – we have some franchisees that don't put in the hours and the effort required. In the current climate,

Botty's Rule No. 23
Working ON your business, not in it!

**No one ever got rich having a lie-in or watching TV –
you've got to work, really hard.**

There is a kind of urban myth that has emerged in recent
times that super-successful people don't work hard. Let
me tell you now that the opposite is true. Super-successful
people work very, very hard. Take a look at Branson's
schedule or Peter Jones or Donald Trump or Duncan
Bannatyne. These guys are passionate about their businesses, and they put in the hours.

My teenage son is trying to prove this rule wrong –
but he will fail! The old American rocker Ted Nugent
articulates this rule really well. In his outspoken book
Ted, White & Blue he says that all you need to succeed
in the twenty-first century is a dream, a dedicated work
ethic and an alarm clock. His premise is that if you want
to get ahead, get up an hour before everybody else.

It's a neat message, and one that I certainly practise
most days of the week. Sorry to burst your bubble on this
one, but that's how it is.

there's no business that can flourish and thrive unless the business owner is working very, very hard at it. There is no short cut and no way around that. Some people try and run multiple businesses, but it's really difficult when there's only one of you. What you end up doing is compromising everywhere and being mediocre at everything. Others are just plain lazy.

Our fourth criteria is that we are looking for 'people' people. More than anything, thebestof is a people business, and if you are someone that energises people, if you've got a happy smile, if people are pleased to see you and enjoy your company, then you will do very well with thebestof – providing you have the other criteria as well, of course. I have got a couple of grumpy franchisees in the business. They're just a bit miserable. While they're doing okay, they could be doing a lot better. Their personality inhibits their growth and is holding them back. They'll never be super-successful because of their attitude, so 'people' people are very important.

Technical Developments

In January 2008, I recruited a new technical director to replace Dave Carruthers. Dave had done a great job, but he had brought thebestof as far as he could with his skill set. Also, his ambitions were as a business owner himself, not as an IT director. So, Nigel Davis joined the team.

It was difficult working with another Nigel (there aren't that many of us, after all), but we managed to find a way to make it work. I've got to be honest: his first year was really horrible. You see, when Dave Carruthers built the original thebestof website back in 2005, he built what I think of as a plumbing system (bear with me on this – I think the analogy works). He built this plumbing system for what we had at the time, which was a two-bedroom starter home, and the plumbing worked really well for a two-bedroom starter home.

What then happened over the intervening three years is that this starter home was extended time and time again. We'd gone out the back; we'd gone up on top as well. It was now a ten-storey skyscraper. Its footprint on the ground was four times the size it was at the beginning, and it had ten times as many bathrooms, but it still had the same plumbing system. It was still the same boiler powering it and, consequently, it couldn't cope. To stretch the analogy still further, when someone turned the shower on in one room, the taps ran dry in another. In short, we had a very unstable website, running on a platform and infrastructure that were inadequate for the complexity of the site and the amount of traffic we were getting. The website kept crashing. It kept falling over, and we knew we had to replace it.

We saw it as an opportunity. We mapped out a new website with a completely different scope. We were going to incorporate lots of new elements into it that would make us a much stronger business, but it took time to develop.

The scope kept creeping, so we kept pushing back the delivery. Two of our key developers left midway through the project. In truth, it was a good thing that they left; we should have waved goodbye to them a few months earlier. The new website, TBO 2.0, was finally delivered in December 2008. It gave us a scalable solution that allows us to cope with anything that the web throws at us in the months and years ahead.

By this point, we were getting over a million unique visitors per month to the website. A lot of our competitors talk about the number of 'hits' that they get. Anyone that talks about hits in terms of web traffic is talking complete bollocks, and they are probably trying to hide something or pull the wool over your eyes. The technical definition of a 'hit' is a request to a web server for a piece of information. On most websites nowadays, certainly ours, the loading of one single page on the site can constitute anywhere between 50 and 120 'hits' because there are a lot of different elements of data on that page. When anyone talks to you about 'hits' on their website, they are really talking about a nonsense figure. Instead, ask them how many 'page views' or 'unique visitors' they get. These are much more useful and meaningful statistics that give you a real sense of how many individual people visited the website in a particular week or month.

Social Media

Not wanting to sit on our laurels, having got the website developed and running smoothly, we got very active with social media. The thing about social media sites such as Twitter, Facebook, etc., is it's where your audience hangs out. There are thousands of people in every town in the UK on Facebook and Twitter right this minute.

From a business perspective, only an idiot would not even try to make contact with these people and connect with them in some way.

Twitter in particular works well for our business. Our franchisees are increasingly utilising it now, some better than others, to get even more business for their customers. If you are strategic in your thinking, and you understand social media properly, it can be a huge benefit to your business.

We've certainly found that to be the case. As well as using social media effectively to promote our own business, it also allows us to shout about and champion our customers on thebestof in a very effective way. It's often easier to shout

Botty's Rule No. 24
Social Media is changing everything.

Thousands of your potential customers, people that live in your area, are on Twitter and Facebook today. You'd have to be either incredibly arrogant or a complete idiot to not even try to connect with them there.

The reality is that social media is, in many ways, a new frontier. It's not like the Internet where search engine optimisation has now, in many cases, been sewn up by individual companies. No one has cracked social media yet. It's completely game on: whatever you do, whatever part of the country you live in, there is the potential for you to get new clients and do new business through the effective use of sites such as Twitter and Facebook.

We've had a lot of success with Twitter in particular over the last 12 months. I can attribute at least £100,000 of sales to Twitter and we've driven over 300,000 people to our websites through it as well. We continue to learn and get better, but it's already making a big difference to our business.

If you're not actively doing this (or have someone doing it on your behalf), then you're almost certainly missing out.

I have some free online training available called 'How to Effectively Grow your Business on Twitter in Less than Six Minutes a Day'. You can access it by joining my Entrepreneurs' Circle on a two-month free trial. You can do that by going to **www.nigel botterill.com/bookoffer** or completing the form at the back of this book.

about someone else than it is to shout about yourself, but you've got to know what you're doing and so many business-people get it wrong. What a lot of people miss with social media is what I call the 'party principle'.

Imagine going to a party, and you don't know anybody there. It's full of strangers. Assuming you want to stay and get involved, how would you behave? Well, you could just sit in the corner and watch; some people do that, but it doesn't make for a very fulfilling party. If you just sit and watch what's happening with social media, then you're not going to reap any benefits from it at all – and neither will you have any fun.

The smart way to behave at a party where you know no one else would be to go and introduce yourself to people. You'd be nice to them, you'd be helpful, you might even try and make them laugh and you'd certainly take an interest in them – you would listen to them. (One of the most powerful lessons my mother ever taught me was that people like to talk about themselves and if you listen, they like you. This is a universal truth, and it's served me well at many parties!)

Of course, to be a real hit at the party you also have to be interesting yourself. Now, most people in business don't get this 'party principle'. You see businesses coming on to Twitter. On day one, they tweet, 'If you want PR, I'm a PR company, here I am.' That's just not the behaviour of someone who's going to have a great party. Imagine turning up at a party, going round to everybody and just talking about you and what you do and asking for business. Some would call that the behaviour of an a*~*hole, and you do meet them at most parties. They're the people that rush around the place only talking about themselves. They're completely self-obsessed. There are lots of business owners using social media like that, and they get ignored, just like they do in the real world.

We've got very good at using social media effectively. We use it properly. We engage with people, we listen to them and we help them. It's played a big part in the development of thebestof over the last couple of years – and my Entrepreneurs' Circle – it is very easy to do if you learn how to do it.

Offers

We introduced offers onto thebestof in autumn 2008. Our rationale here is that very few businesses make good offers to their customers. Yet, those that do and do it well have a lot of success with them. We wanted to encourage local businesses (our customers) to make offers because we knew that it would enable us to get a lot more business for them.

In addition, if, in order to access the offers, local people have to register with us, then we would be building our database of local people that we could further market our member businesses to and we'd also be able to track exactly how much business we were sending to those member businesses.

But a lot of businesses were reticent to provide offers for us to use – some still are. These business owners are stuck in

Botty's Rule No. 25
Good offers make you money ...

... Don't just slash your margins.

So many business owners are reluctant to implement offers, and when they do, it's a straightforward sale with X per cent off. But there are much more creative offers available to any business that can have a much more positive impact on your P&L.

A Chinese restaurant near me ran a great offer last year. It was for a free Coke and won-ton with every order over £30. The offer was introduced into their takeaway business and when I got talking to the owner, she explained that they knew that their average takeaway spend was £27 (just knowing this immediately propels them into the top 5% of restaurant owners), and they wanted to do something that could push this up above £30. So they went down to their cash-and-carry to see what was on offer there. They were able to get a large number of one-litre bottles of Coke – and this offer was created.

The impact was startling. Not only did the average spend go up to just over £33 (that's a 20% uplift) but the number of takeaway orders they received also went up – by over 15%. This was because the three other Chinese restaurants in the area didn't have the nous to have their own offer, so people came to get their free Coke and won-tons rather than going to the other places. This compounded impact of an increase in transaction volume and an increase in transaction size had a significant impact on the profitability of the takeaway business.

There's an offer of this power and magnitude waiting to be uncovered in your business.

the dark ages; they are not adapting to the changing economic environment nor to the changes in society. The fact is that people are a lot more discerning now, and you have to work harder than ever before as a business owner to persuade people to spend their money with you. Good offers can play a big part in that.

Other business owners are just dead lazy with their offers. The classic lazy man's offer is 10% off. Let me tell you, '10% off' just doesn't work anymore. People are immune to it. Go on, be honest, when did you last get excited over a '10% off' offer? It doesn't drive behaviour.

It's also not smart from a business perspective, because 10% off your price equates to 20%, 30% or more off your profit. So you're slashing your margins and you're buying turnover at the expense of profit, which is bad thing to do.

We encourage our thebestof business owners to get creative with their ideas. We help them think about offers that will make them money, not cost them money. This is so important in this new economy. Getting new customers and keeping them coming back is getting harder but good offers can play a big part in that – which is why we profile them and push them via thebestof.

We've also just introduced our thebestof app, which pushes local offers to people's mobile phones, so you've always got the current offers from your best local businesses on your mobile.

'14 Days of Love' – and Membership

One of the most exciting things in recent times on thebestof has been our '14 Days of Love' initiative, which people may have seen around the UK during the first two weeks in February, in the run-up to Valentine's Day.

We ran it for the first time in 2010 and the concept came about as a result of an initiative that Apple ran for their iPhone customers in the UK over Christmas 2009. They ran a campaign called 12 Days of Christmas and for 12 days after Christmas, each day every iPhone customer got an opportunity to have a free download of something from Apple, whether it was a song, a video clip, an application or a game.

My teenage son Cameron is a complete Applephile and we were on holiday in Florida during the promotional period. As 7 p.m. approached (i.e., 12 a.m. in the UK), we'd usually be in a restaurant having our evening meal and Cameron would be eagerly waiting for midnight to tick over in the UK so the next gift became available for his iPhone.

I thought it would be brilliant if I could have people eagerly waiting for the next day on my website. It just got me thinking, and I came up with an idea. Rather than the 12 Days of Christmas, we could do 14 Days of Love with thebestof. I came back from the holiday on 5 January 2010, and we launched 14 Days of Love nationwide on 1 February.

We had 26 days in which to take this from conception to delivery and my team did an amazing job.

The idea was that for 14 days, culminating on Valentine's Day, we would encourage the people of the UK to show some love for their favourite local businesses. That's what the whole campaign was about.

We explained that their favourite local businesses had been there for them throughout the snow and the storms of the winter, through the banking crisis and the credit crunch and the recession; day after day, they work hard, serving their customers, and we suggested that people should just take a moment out of their day to tell their favourite local business that they really appreciate what they do – they should 'show some love'. Of course, the best way to do that is via our website, or via postcards that we provided.

We had a big web campaign, and we got loads of media interest as well.

We put the 'Love-o-meter'™ together so we could show the best-loved businesses in each town on the website – these were the businesses that were getting the most love from their customers. We had a 'Love-o-meter' by business type as well, so we could show the most-loved pet-grooming business in the UK, say, or the most-loved accountants.

We also had a third 'Love-o-meter' which showed the top 100 best-loved businesses in the UK.

Everybody that got involved and 'shared some love' was eligible to claim a free badge that said 'I'm a great lover.' They were very popular!

Lots of businesses got really engaged with the whole campaign. It was good for them, it got them energised and excited and it engaged their customers. It was good for us, too: it built our membership numbers, it built our relationships with our businesses, and it generated a shedload of media coverage as well.

On the day it launched, I did 29 separate radio interviews, which were featured on 103 different radio stations. The power of the press and media can help businesses hugely if you give them a good story. This one was perfect for local radio and local newspapers.

As the '14 Days of Love' campaign drew to a close, we were all set to be featured on *The One Show* on BBC One at 7 p.m., but unfortunately, we got pulled at the last minute. Another story came up, so they dropped us. It was a real shame, because we were all geared up, and it would have been tremendous publicity for us. Nonetheless, '14 Days of Love' helped thebestof hugely. It raised our profile, grew our membership, got lots more businesses on board and injected a real 'feel-good' factor among our franchisees and everyone else that got involved. It was also brilliant fun.

Being able to connect with local people makes a huge difference to the power of the marketing that thebestof can do for our customers, the local businesses. For instance, my franchisee in Bromsgrove in Worcestershire is a guy named Ian Prowse. Ian is a great guy. He was one of the very first thebestof franchisees, and he's built a fab business in what is a very modest-sized town (population 20,000) just south of Birmingham. More than 5,000 Bromsgrove residents have now registered with thebestof, which means that Ian has the names and email addresses of almost 25% of the population of the town. Now, that's significant because he can communicate with them, and he does regularly and that communication makes Ian the most powerful marketer in his town – bar none. No one else can offer business such relevant, laser-like market-ing and this development of our membership numbers has become a very strategic push for thebestof in recent times. It's putting us in a very strong competitive position, so we can really deliver for our customers.

Video

We've introduced video to thebestof website in the spring of 2010, and it's working tremendously well. The arrival of YouTube and programmes like *You've Been Framed* have turned everybody into broadcasters. You can explain a lot more about a business and get a much better sense of what it's like in a one-minute video than you can through reading 500 words of text and seeing a few pictures – which is why we've pioneered the way for local businesses to incorporate video into their marketing through thebestof. We do a lot of stuff with our own video cameras, as well as providing a professional filming and editing option. I reckon most people prefer the videos that look slightly 'homemade' and not too slick. The realism makes them endearing.

We're already seeing some tremendous videos, and it's working very well for the businesses that are getting involved – making their phones ring with new customers and growing their sales. We're on a mission now to try and feature video for as many of our businesses as we possibly can because we know it will help them to grow.

Call Tracking Numbers

Another important element of thebestof proposition is 'tracking numbers'. This was another strategic play that makes us further unique amongst marketing companies. What we found a year or so ago is that we were starting to lose a few customers from thebestof. We haven't lost many at all over the years as our retention rate is really high, but a few started to leave us. When we enquired as to why, they were telling us that they weren't getting any business through thebestof. Thing is, we knew that was wrong.

We could see the number of people we had sent to their websites. We knew, in some instances, that we had guided people to them directly (one of the most valuable elements of thebestof proposition is 'mix & match', where our franchisees, who spend all their days out and about meeting people around town, introduce customers directly to a business. 'Oh, you need a new fence, do you, well you must speak to Mr X, he's the best fencer in town, here's his number ...'). One thebestof business in Leeds had my parents come in and buy new carpets from him. They told him that they had found him on thebestof. Yet six months later he swore blind that not a single customer had come in mentioning thebestof.

In short, local businesses are very bad at accurately tracking where their business comes from. We thought that it wasn't sensible to put ourselves and the future of our business in their hands, as it were. We wanted to know if there was a way around that.

Our franchisee consultation group, which is a group of our top performing franchisees that meets three times a year to help plan and map the strategic direction for the business, came up with a solution to this problem – tracking numbers.

We now encourage all our franchisees to put tracking numbers on every business that they champion and promote. A tracking number is a unique local phone number that rings on the business's existing phone line, but it allows us to see exactly how many calls the business has received as a result of our marketing efforts.

Botty's Rule No. 26
Only lazy, incompetent business owners don't know how well each bit of their marketing works ...

There's an old saying from the 1930s that says, 'I know half my marketing works and half doesn't ... I just don't know which is which.'

Eighty years ago that phrase had validity, but it is complete nonsense in the twenty-first century. If you don't know what returns you're getting from pretty much every piece of your marketing, it's because you haven't been bothered to do so. One great tool that you should be using is **tracking numbers**.

These are a brilliant invention. Your phone line and phone number are set exactly as it is now but you purchase additional phone numbers (these are local numbers; they don't have to be 0845 or 0800, for instance) and they simply sit on top of your existing phone line. Your staff answer the phone in the same way. Nothing changes.

'OK, Nige, what's the big deal, then?' I hear you say. Well, you can log online, 24/7, and see exactly how many times each of these tracking phone numbers has been called. Not only that, but you can see who called the number, the time and whether the call was answered.

This works best if you only use each number in one specific place. For example, if you advertise in the local paper, you have one specific tracking number that you only use for that so when people call on that number, it's clear where they've got it from. You do the same thing with your website, your business cards, with every advertising media that you utilise. This way you get to know what's made your phone ring. It's really powerful, potent stuff – yet so few businesses use it.

It's made a massive difference to our business. When I introduced tracking numbers for the first time over two years ago, I discovered that we were missing an average of over 40 phone calls a week that were coming into our sales lines between 5 and 6 p.m. Our receptionist was switching our phones onto the night service when she went home, yet I had staff there till 6 p.m., and they could take the calls. Conservatively that's been worth over £60,000 to me in the last 12 months.

By the way, the advertising salespeople hate these tracking numbers because it makes them accountable. They won't tell you about them because they don't want you to know about them and use them. That should tell you something on its own! Incidentally, we've been encouraging all our franchisees of thebestof to utilise tracking numbers for over 18 months now. We want to put a tracking number on every thebestof business so we can know exactly how many times we're making their phone ring. We know we do a fantastic job, and we're keen to demonstrate it to our customers.

We can also see if they're answering those calls because when we put this in place, we found, amazingly, that lots of businesses don't answer all their calls when people ring them up!

Now we can prove that we're making their phone ring. As a direct result of tracking numbers we've been able to help businesses in other ways, too. Those that had call answering problems have been able to fix it. We had one vet surgery in South London getting over 60 calls a month through thebestof but only answering 45 of them. That's a lot of missed opportunities that the vet had no idea about. With our help, he was able to fix that.

Special Savings on Tracking Numbers

Whatever business you're in, I recommend you deploy tracking numbers on all of your marketing. No advertising salesperson will ever tell you about it because once you use tracking numbers, every piece of your marketing becomes accountable – which is why it's one of the neatest tricks open to business owners right now. The company I use for all my tracking numbers is City Numbers. It's run by Craig Busst, and they do a great job. I highly recommend them. Craig has agreed to a special tariff for all readers of *Botty's Rules*, which makes tracking numbers even more of a bargain – and they were dead cheap already before he agreed to even more discounts! You can access those special prices online at: **www.citynumbers.co.uk/nigel**.

We've also introduced 'Quote Me Local'. People can go onto thebestof website and request quotes directly from businesses for work. It makes it very easy for local people to get access to the best local tradespeople and suppliers.

We've continued to develop our print elements as well, because thebestof is very definitely not just a website. It's meant that thebestof has become a complete marketing solution for great local businesses, and it's amazing value too.

At the heart of thebestof are our franchisees. Everything hangs off them. They're at the centre of their local business communities, and when they operate their business well, which very many of them do, they're able to help the best local businesses hugely as well as adding immense value to their local community. It's a really brilliant business for everyone involved, and I'm very proud to be part of it.

CHAPTER 12
EXPLOSIVE MARKETING

We have a lot of restaurants as customers on thebestof, and I meet a lot of them as I travel around the country. One thing becomes clear when you spend time with lots of restaurant owners – most of them are rubbish at marketing their restaurant. I mean, really bad. I would suggest that restaurants are probably the worst sector of any that we deal with on thebestof, when it comes to marketing. There are exceptions, of course. Some restaurant owners do a great job and are very switched on, but they are very much the exception and not the rule.

Botty's Rule No. 27
Your most valuable asset – bar none – is your database.

It's not your customers' job to remember to do business with you. It's your job to remind them … and that's why your database is so important.

I've got a very large database now. There are over 400,000 people on it. It's taken me seven years to build and compile, and I've spent a lot of money collecting leads to nourish and nurture my database. It is, by a country mile, the most valuable thing I possess. You see, every time I send an email out to my database, I make sales. Every time. Do you have any idea what that does to your peace of mind, to your quality of sleep, to your ability to plan ahead with certainty for your business? It's a truly wonderful thing to have, and this applies in any business.

With our Explosive Marketing system, we help restaurants build their database, and then we work their database for them. Surprise, surprise, customers that previously were dining with the restaurant two or three times a year now come back four, five or six times a year. That increase in frequency has an exponential impact on profitability.

Build your database, keep in regular contact with your customers and prospects and you'll make (a lot) more sales. It's that straightforward.

As my football coach used to say to me when I was a kid, 'Simple things, done well, look good.' The bit he missed is that they make you a lot of money as well!

Typically, restaurant owners have no control over who comes in their establishment. They open the doors every day and pretty much hope for the best. They never try and collect their customers' contact information, for instance. Think about it – if people that are dining in a restaurant today have a good experience, there's a reasonable chance that they may come back another time, especially if you remind them or make them an offer and give them a reason return.

Yet, most restaurant owners rarely attempt to get any contact information, and those that do collect data hardly ever use it to communicate with their customers. It's not your customers' job to remember to come back and do business with you, it's your job to remind them, particularly if you're in a restaurant business.

All It Takes Is a Nudge

This was really brought home to me in December 2008. I got a Christmas card from the Knowle Indian Brasserie, a restaurant near to where we live. This is an Indian restaurant that Sue and I used to go to quite regularly a few years ago. They serve very nice, high-quality Indian food, they're local and we enjoyed going there. But for no good reason at all, we just got out of the habit of visiting the Knowle Indian Brasserie.

We never had a bad experience there or anything like that, but we started going to other Indian restaurants – after all, there are several near our home. In short, until that December, we hadn't eaten at the Knowle Indian Brasserie for over three years. Then I got this card from them. Inside was a message that explained that the restaurant had recently been refurbished and that they'd love it if we visited to see the new decor. To help persuade us, a £10 voucher was included in the card. They gave us a nudge!

As it happened, a couple of days later, Sue and I had a babysitter lined up. We were going out for dinner and a movie, so where do you think we went? Knowle Indian Brasserie. Now, to be clear, there is absolutely no way we would have gone to that restaurant had we not had that little nudge. They had gone off our radar, until we got the nudge. It was that £10 voucher, and it drew us in that night.

So few restaurants do this as they have no database. Those that have a database never use it. They very rarely make offers. They leave so much of their business success down to chance or some misplaced belief that by running a restaurant that serves great food, has good service and a nice ambience, they'll be successful. They won't – not nowadays with so much choice available.

Success, for the vast majority of restaurants, comes down to the effectiveness of their marketing.

It was clear that a lot of restaurant owners needed help. What they love is running a fab restaurant. They're not expert at marketing – but at N5 we are. I felt sure there was a business opportunity here, so I sat down with one of my colleagues, Mark Creaser, who had joined the business a couple of years earlier.

Mark's a very bright guy – very switched on. He initially joined me in a sales role, but it became very clear quite quickly that he had a lot more to offer than just pure sales. I felt that this restaurant marketing business that I was conceiving was going to be a really great opportunity for him to really show what he could do and deliver real value for my business. Together, we started to map out a completely 'done-for-you' marketing system for restaurants.

It's Not Rocket Science

We figured that we'd have to start by helping restaurants to build their database. So we created 'VIP' membership cards for their customers. To get a card, people had to give the restaurant their information. Then, every time the customers came in, if they used their membership card, we'd be able to track the transactions and they would earn loyalty points. When they got a certain number of loyalty points, they'd qualify for a reward.

Now, this is hardly rocket science. Loyalty schemes have been around for a long time and they are an integral part of some of the most successful businesses in the UK – Tesco and Boots, for instance.

What Tesco and Boots do, of course, that is really smart, is that they use their loyalty scheme as a communication tool with their customers – so that's what we set out to do with our system.

We called it the Explosive Marketing system and what the system does is use the restaurants data to keep in touch with their customers on their behalf.

When people sign up for their free VIP membership card, we ask them for their birthday, their wedding anniversary, their wife's birthday, that sort of thing. We then use all these different occasions to communicate with them and nudge them back into the restaurant. There are other events throughout the year like Valentine's Day or Halloween or Mother's Day, for example, that we use as well – all to give people that nudge. And let me tell you, it works like a dream!

Mark and I began to develop the system. We sourced the membership cards (all of which are designed for each restaurant) and the point-of-sales terminals (so we can track transactions and customers can earn loyalty points, as every time they dine at the restaurant their card is swiped in the point-of-sale terminal) and we designed some eye-catching, very different postcards, full of vibrant colour.

On an anniversary postcard, which we send out during their anniversary month, as well as the restaurant logo, there is an image of their first name carved into the top of a cork and their initial on the top of the wire champagne cork holder. How do you think the customer feels when he or she gets this postcard from a local restaurant? This postcard gets, on average, a 31% response.

Similarly, we have a personalised birthday postcard range, and we get an extraordinarily high response rate of people coming back in the restaurant during their birthday month; the average response is over 23%. Not everybody comes in with their birthday offer, but we don't give up straight away. If they don't use their birthday postcard, then they'll receive a card the following month. People love this one, and it has a response rate above 20%.

Some restaurants want to attract new customers as well as get their existing ones coming back more often. Our 'new mover' card does that for them. We source data of people that have moved house into streets close to the restaurant and then send them out a 'Welcome' card. The offer on the back is usually a 'double points on your next visit', providing you come in the next month. It drives customers back into the restaurant much more quickly than they otherwise would have come, meaning more profit and busier tables for the restaurant owner.

We have cards for Mother's Day, for Halloween, and we have dubbed February 'Romance' month, personalising our postcards with love hearts. We have postcards to try to get diners who only come in for dinner to go to the restaurant for lunch, postcards for people who haven't been in for a while ... the possibilities are endless, fun and exciting for everyone involved. And our use of whizzy technology and good design to deliver powerful personalisation has helped the Explosive Marketing system deliver stunning results for the restaurants that we work with.

Multiple Media Increases Response

As well as the postcards, we communicate with people regularly through email, by letter and by SMS text messaging and, of course, everything is done for the restaurants. They don't lift a finger. Their only job is to get their existing diners to complete the VIP member form when they come in. They then just send those forms to us, we input them into the database and do everything else. It's database marketing at its finest.

What we've found is that by using multiple media (e.g., postcards plus email plus letter plus text message), we get a much better response. There's a lesson there for every business owner, whatever sector you are in.

The Explosive Marketing system is topped off by providing restaurants with a detailed monthly report that gives them complete transparency. These management reports are really powerful. They contain the sort of information that all business owners would love to have available to them every month, and they are very comprehensive.

On the front page it shows clearly what the return on investments has been for the restaurant in the past month. We're very open about the return on investment that the system is generating for our customers. We want long-term relationships with them, so we share everything.

We explain how much they spent on Explosive that month and let them know how much this amount generated this much in sales and exactly what their return on investment was. Then we explain that for every £1 spent, they earned £X.

Typically, restaurants get between 400%–1,000% return on investment each month, which means that for every £1 they spend, they're getting between £4–10 back.

Inside the management report, we break down exactly what's happened in the past month with their marketing. We tell them who their top 20 most valuable customers are, and how to call them. We let them know the quality of their data, what marketing activity is planned for the next month and a whole load of other useful stuff.

What we've found surprising, though, is that many restaurant owners don't even look at the management reports! But that's not our problem. It's important that we send it, and it's important that we are completely transparent in sharing this useful and important information with them.

Of course, we look at the reports every month to identify any problems so we can work with the restaurant to put it right. What we found quite early on was that one of the biggest problems was that, in some restaurants, staff were not swiping the membership cards through the point-of-sale terminal (POS) when diners were coming in. Now, obviously, what this means is that there is no revenue being attached to the marketing that's going on. For instance, we were sending postcards out for someone's birthday, and they would come in and show the postcard to the waiter. The waiter was taking the voucher but not putting it through our point-of-sale system, so there was no indication that this was a sale as a result of Explosive Marketing.

We were getting restaurants that were spending £500–600 in a month and appearing to get no customers back in. Now, because the numbers were zero, it was clear that there was a problem. We had to put a little hit squad on the road, travelling the country and training restaurant staff and making sure that they entered every transaction so that the restaurant owner got accurate information and, of course, their customers earned their loyalty points.

Key Partners

Building a system like Explosive and pulling all the different bits together, so that it works seamlessly and automatically for the restaurants, is actually not as straightforward as it might seem. You need partners in the right areas.

We have experts working with us in print management, people managing the data, the point-of-sale terminals that collect the transactions and the loyalty software. There are designers, plastic card producers, mailing and fulfilment houses, email servers, text providers and more. In short, there's a lot of complexity to building a product like this, not to mention the kind of marketing knowledge needed to deploy it properly.

Consequently, it took Mark and I almost 12 weeks of dedicated, focused effort to build Explosive from scratch. Once we had it, we embarked on the launch in spring of 2009.

Once again, we used a series of events to launch our product. Initially, we planned to do 10 events around the country. We involved a lot of our franchisees in thebestof, and they were inviting their customers, the restaurant owners, but what quickly became clear is that a lot of these restaurant owners wouldn't travel very far. They would travel 5–10 miles, but they wouldn't travel 40–50 miles. This was a really big issue and we found that restaurant owners were not coming to our launch events, not because they weren't interested, but because it was an hour's drive away.

This was really frustrating, particularly in difficult economic times. I couldn't understand why business owners wouldn't take more responsibility to do a bit more to better themselves and learn new things. This was completely alien to me. I thought nothing of jumping on a plane and flying to Dallas or Denver to learn some new stuff, but a lot of restaurant owners weren't prepared to do 40 miles on the M5. But that was how it was. We had to adjust to it. There was no point in fighting it, so we readjusted our schedule and ended up doing 29 events in 15 days!

For three weeks, we did two events a day. We got restaurant managers in, and I presented a 90-minute presentation. The first half of it explained in layperson's terms why restaurants were so rubbish at marketing and what they should be doing. I created some real pain for them in that part of the session. Then, when they were squirming in their seats, I presented the solution that would fix everything for them … with hardly any effort or work on their part.

We had a good offer that gave them a real incentive to sign up on the day and we got dozens and dozens of restaurants on board, which got the business moving, with traction, straightaway.

Telesales Selection

Having done our three-week UK tour, the next step was to hire a sales team. We put three sales staff on the road (all hired via Meta-Morphose, so all were young, hungry, bright gradu-ates with good propensity to sell) and deployed telemarketing support to get them appointments. The telemarketing was interesting, by the way, because most businesses, I suspect, would just find a telesales company, ask them to make some calls and hope for the best to see what results they get. What we actually did was ask three companies to make calls, and I gave them all portions of a single data set.

We carved 1,500 prospects into three and gave them 500 prospects each. They all had three days' worth of calling to get us appointments on this data set. I was, basically, doing a trial to see which of the companies was best. They all knew the situation; I was very open with them.

What happened was dramatic. One of the telemarketing companies did twice as well as the other two. The company that performed best was my 'third favourite' from when I'd first met them.

By the way, our top performer is just an individual lady who calls from her house, but she's great at it. She completely outperformed her rivals.

Now, if I'd gone with one of the other two companies, I wouldn't have realised that it was possible to get results that were twice as good. You do need to be smart in how you deploy telemarketing. Having done the trial, the performance standard had been set.

I adopted this approach because of my experience with CPP many years earlier. I knew that telemarketing is a very fickle business and success depends on three things.

1. **The biggest single factor is the person making the calls.**
   If you get that wrong, your results will never be good. The individual does matter. They matter a lot, which is what we proved with our test.

2. **The second factor will be the proposition of whatever it is that you are selling.**
    It's always much easier to sell appointments than it is to sell products on the telephone, and that's what we did here. We were filling the diary of our salespeople.
3. **The third element that will affect your success with telemarketing is the quality of your data.**
    You need to know if you are calling the right prospects at the right time. We were able to get our hands on some good data.

We used a lot of direct mail to support our telemarketing activity, which can be another big factor in determining success.

We were putting out some quite creative mail pieces that were going to restaurant owners to create some awareness. Again, it's that big lesson about the use of multiple types of media and multiple communications. Just because people don't respond the first time they hear from you doesn't mean they don't want what you've got! Everybody is busy. You've got to repeatedly communicate with people in order to create awareness and get your message across. That's what we do, and we do it well.

We've added a couple of major enhancements to the Explosive Marketing system in 2010. The best one is that every time a VIP member dines in the restaurant, we send them a short email the following day, asking for feedback on their meal. They simply click a link in the email and fill in a short survey. The result is that the restaurant owner now receives objective, honest feedback on a consistent basis and we show the feedback in a graph in the management report each month.

It's very hard for business owners to get consistent, honest, objective feedback from their customers, particularly in a restaurant. If the owner walks the tables, then they might find out about the big problems, but they won't find out what people are really thinking – not in Britain, we're too inhibited!

These surveys are gold dust for restaurant owners. They happen automatically, with no effort at all on their part. They receive a detailed picture of exactly what their customers think. It's powerful stuff that gives them a huge edge in their market.

Explosive is now a great business. Having played a key part in building it, Mark now runs that business for me, and he's put in place a high-quality team to support him.

We've started to get enquiries from other sectors outside the restaurant market, so we're now embarking on taking Explosive into other sectors where we can see huge potential to help a lot of business owners through what is bound to be a fairly tough time in the next few years.

On reflection, I believe that the Explosive Marketing product and service is the best single product I've ever been involved in. It really is superb in every way. It's well thought through, completely comprehensive and very well delivered. Most importantly, it delivers great results for our customers!

If you run a restaurant – or any other business – and you'd like to find out more about the Explosive Marketing system, visit **www.ExplosiveMarketing.co.uk**.

Update

In April 2011 I agreed to sell Explosive Marketing in much the same way as had happened with *Raring2Go!* almost three years earlier. I received an offer I couldn't refuse from one of our key strategic partners who had been involved with Explosive since its inception.

CHAPTER 13
PRIVATE ENTREPRENEURS' CIRCLE

It all started with a big mistake.

You may remember that around Christmas 2008 the media in the UK were at their gloomiest. They could not pour enough misery onto our TV screens and into our newspapers. It was all about the recession. We were all doomed, the world was about to end ... It was a very miserable time for anyone in business.

As Christmas approached, I felt that, as a responsible franchisor, I ought to do something to help thebestof franchisees to handle what was going on. I wanted to give them some tangible support and techniques so that they could enter the New Year on the front foot with a bounce in their step and continue the growth of their business despite the economic downturn. There was lots of opportunity for them. Our product was better than ever; we were offering way better value for a lot less money than traditional established marketing methods. The number of businesses using our services was growing month on month. There were a lot of reasons to feel positive, and I wanted to make sure our franchisees were in a good place.

I decided to put on a couple of what I called 'Recession Training' events for thebestof franchisees. I set the dates as the first two working days of 2009, so I could get them up and running straight into the New Year.

We've got our own bespoke training suite at our offices in Solihull that holds 60 people. It's in use most days because we do a lot of training. That room was full for that first 'Recession Training' event and though I say so myself, it went very well – much better than I thought it would.

The following day when the second bunch of franchisees came down, we had another great session. This time, as the franchisees left the building at the end of the day, I had one of my team waiting, with a video camera, asking for their comments on how the day had gone. Overnight, he pulled together a really nice video with our franchisees saying how great this course was and how everybody should come to it.

You see, while 120 franchisees had benefitted from the course over the two days, that meant I had another 130 franchisees that hadn't yet experienced it. Given that it had gone so well, I thought I ought to try and help them out, too. So I asked my team to send an email out to those 130 franchisees that hadn't yet been on the course. I wanted to send a link to the video with a message that said something like, 'Look, don't just take our word for it; you really ought to come on this course. Here's what your fellow franchisees say …'

Unfortunately, they made a mistake. Rather than sending the email to 130 franchisees, they actually sent it to the 21,000 customers of those 130 franchisees. This was a big cock-up, but it was compounded half an hour later. When they realised what they'd done, they sent a second email that said, 'I'm really sorry. That earlier email wasn't meant for you … Please don't watch the video – it was just for our franchisees.'

Well, of course, what happened is that everybody clicked on the link to the video.

That email went out on Friday afternoon, and I got a call from Andy Hurst late afternoon on Saturday. He asked if I had seen what happened to our video on YouTube. I hadn't. He said, 'Well, it's gone bananas!' Sure enough it had over 10,000 views, which was ridiculous because it was only meant to have been sent to 130 people.

We came in on Monday morning to over 1,000 emails. Among those messages, a couple of people were a bit upset, but most of them were just saying, 'These things happen, hope you don't get into trouble.' But 46 people had emailed us saying, 'This training sounds great ... can I come on it?'

Never one to miss an opportunity, I called a meeting of my management team, and we decided that we'd put this training on for businesses as well as for our franchisees. We set four dates and sent an email out that day. All we did in total was send out three emails . We didn't market the four events any other way and 600 business owners booked a ticket, paying £100 each.

It was a huge success. The businesses loved the training. It reinforced their relationships with thebestof and we made a bit of money as well. It was a win-win-win situation.

There's a big lesson there – out of crisis comes opportunity. There was a silver lining. It would have been really easy for us to go into crisis mode, but because we responded quickly, it worked out. That's another huge lesson: speed matters. One of the reasons so many people booked on the course was because of the speed at which we responded and took action.

Because the events went so well, I got a lot of requests to do more. I enjoyed doing them and they were helping the business on so many levels, so in the summer of 2009 we did a second series of events. This time we had 10 dates. We called this event 'Screw Surviving'.

This time, well over a thousand businesses came along. It

Botty's Rule No. 28
Speed matters.

There was just five weeks between me deciding to develop and launch My Mag and us actually launching it.

My Little Wrapper had a six-week gestation period. That's all.

When Sue launched the Dickens Heath Directory, it was less than 24 hours from making the decision to do it to getting her first customer on board and the first cheque in the bank.

These are not lucky stories; they are illustrations of a key facet of success in business in the twenty-first century because speed really does matter.

If you're going to do anything, much better to do it quickly.

That way, if it fails, you can move onto the next thing and you have not wasted big chunks of your life on it or, conversely, if it's successful, then you can tap into that success much more quickly, and it allows you to do other things more quickly as a result.

Slow in business is invariably bad, yet it's where most people are most comfortable and that, again, is one of the reasons why most people don't achieve the success that they aspire to – because they just don't get enough things done quickly enough.

was simple messages – stuff that was obvious to me about what businesses should be doing to stave off and fight the economic downturn, but it wasn't obvious to all the delegates.

Commitment to Learning

I started to realise that I actually know a ton of stuff. The reason I know so much is because of the ongoing commitment that I make to learning new things. I did a bit of investigation, and I worked out that I've actually spent £244,167 in the five years to 2009 on summits, boot camps, Info Products, online courses, books and everything else.

I'm a Diamond member of the Glazer-Kennedy Insider Circle, which is something that I take a huge amount of learning from on a monthly basis. I was part of Bill Glazer's Mastermind Group, which involved flying across to America three times a year to sit round a boardroom table with 15 other like-minded entrepreneurs. It was probably the single most valuable thing I've ever done.

Anyone who has read Napoleon Hill's book, *Think and Grow Rich*, will remember how much importance he places on being part of what he calls a mastermind group. This is where a group of 10–16 people get together to mutually support each other. If you get the right mix of people with the right expertise, it can be hugely beneficial to everybody.

Bill used to chair our meetings, and we all paid Bill a very large sum of money to be part of that group, but it was an absolute snip at the price because of the value we all got from it. We would sit around the boardroom table for two days and spend 60–90 minutes focusing on each other's businesses. I used to get more value from the slots where we talked about other people's businesses than I did in the bits that we talked about my own. I learnt so much.

One of my frustrations during the 'Screw Surviving' events was this realisation that people wanted a lot more of me. I got a lot of emails and requests at the end of those meetings from people wanting help and advice, but I had no products or service to provide.

I also began to understand that my energy, enthusiasm and my passion for business were inspiring to others. Someone pointed out to me that most of the people offering advice and guidance to business owners in the UK haven't 'done it'. They're teaching from textbooks, not from real life, whereas I've actually done it – and am doing it still.

It took someone else to point out to me how completely unique it is that I have built five separate £1-million-plus businesses in five years, all from scratch.

Botty's Rule No. 29
The single biggest thing you can do ...

If you analyse my business and much of what I talk about in this book, then what you will find is very little of what we have done has been original. The one fortunate thing I had when I set up my own business was a deep sense of my own inadequacy and a desire to learn ... fast. I knew that I was ill equipped to run my own business, so I made it my business to study and learn from the best people in the world and to learn all the different elements and things that I needed to do.

As I've said, In the last five years alone, I've spent over £244,000 on learning. I make a firm commitment each year to learn and develop my own set of knowledge and skills. What I then do is replicate the stuff that works that I've learnt. That's been absolutely critical to the dramatic growth of our business.

What was pointed out to me six months ago is that very few business owners make this commitment to learning. Similarly, very few business owners achieve the level of success that they set out to achieve when they went into business. This isn't a coincidence. These two facts are linked. There's a direct correlation between people's commitment to finding and following proven success strategies and their eventual level of success. A direct link.

Another person, this time a franchisee, suggested to me that I actually had a responsibility to share my learning with other business owners.

It was a real big lesson for me – most business owners don't commit to learning, and most business owners don't enjoy the success that they set out to achieve with their business. That is not a coincidence. The two facts are directly related.

And if that wasn't enough, around that time I found I'd won another national award – this time the 'Essence of the Entrepreneur' award from BT. The judges said some very complimentary things about me and my prize was to be photographed by top fashion photographer Perou. The picture was meant to reflect my business so, understandably I guess, he went down 'the best of' route. My picture was taken on a freezing day on Acton Common in West London. It took over an hour, I popped nine bottles of very cheap Cava in order to get the shot and I have no idea who the other two guys in the photo with me were. They were paid extras, bless 'em. Oooh the glamour!

So Much Stuff …

So, given that it seemed that there was a demand for my expertise, I decided I would launch something that would enable me to help other UK business owners to flourish, thrive and make their businesses much bigger. I knuckled down and mapped out how we were going to do this.

What my management team and I decided is that I would devote 25% of my time to teaching, coaching and mentoring UK business owners who wanted to succeed and grow. We'd fulfil it under the banner of 'Nigel Botterill's Entrepreneurs' Circle'.

Now, in putting the Entrepreneurs' Circle together, I was determined to provide people with exactly what they needed.

I knew they were going to need regular, little injections of information. One of the best ways we can do that is by sending them something in the post every month, so we produce a publication that we call *The Entrepreneur's Circular*.

This is typically a 20- or 24-page magazine. It's full of very sharp, hard-hitting and incisive information. One member has described it as getting 'a seminar through the post' each month.

In the same envelope as the circular, members receive a 'success template'. This takes a different marketing concept or idea each month and lays all out step-by-step, so they can just implement it straight away.

We needed a way for people to get their specific questions answered, so I do interactive Q&A sessions each month. These are recorded and made available as podcasts. We do online webinars with experts and leaders in different fields.

There's a range of online training material available to people, including full courses on how to use Twitter effectively to grow your business and how to drive sales using Google AdWords.

Every fortnight, there's a two-hour period when members can ring me directly, and I'll answer the phone. I had a special 'bat-phone' installed just for this purpose. They get 10 minutes, and I help them with a particular challenge or obstacle in their business.

The single most popular part of the Entrepreneurs' Circle is NB-TV. We broadcast one programme on Wednesday each week. The programmes are 'bite-sized bits to help your business grow' and they are all fronted by me, often from a famous venue or interesting place. I've filmed episodes recently from Wimbledon and Lords, a baseball match in Dallas and the TT circuit on the Isle of Man.

Each episode is less than five minutes long and contains a single, focused message that members can apply to their businesses. I have great fun filming the episodes and they usually make people smile. Most importantly I know, from all the great feedback, that they're making a real difference to people's businesses.

However, the best and most useful part of the Entrepreneurs' Circle is, without a doubt, our monthly full-day events, which take place in a different part of the country each month. The events are very well attended, with over 100 people typically at each meeting, and we spend time fixing businesses. We run 'Hot Seats' and deal with all the questions and issues and challenges that people are facing. They are very practical events. I love doing them and people seem to enjoy coming and, crucially, get a lot out of it.

When taken together, all these different elements of the Entrepreneurs' Circle provide a really comprehensive set of support mechanisms for business owners. It is delivered by someone who has 'been there and done that', and people seem to respond well to that.

I'm really enjoying helping other UK business owners to develop their businesses, and we're making a big difference to many of them. It's very fulfilling.

Members can use all the elements of the Circle or they can pick and choose which bits are most useful and appropriate for them. But, of course, they do have to do something with all this stuff if it's to have any lasting benefit.

People have to take ownership and responsibility themselves and take action.

Action is key. If they do that, and they are committed to learning and developing their skills, then I've got a lot that I can teach people that can really help their business to grow much much faster and that's what we've set out to do.

It really fuels my tank when I receive emails from members of the Entrepreneurs' Circle telling me how stuff that I've provided them with has helped them. Often it's only a small, little thing, but it's made a huge impact to their business, and to their P&L. It's very fulfilling.

We're going to continue to develop and grow the Entrepreneurs' Circle in the years ahead. We've got a number of plans for it that will make it bigger and better and more influential. It's been described by others as something that 'Every UK business owner should be part of.' Certainly, we're going to focus on delivering value, help and assistance to any UK business owner that is serious about developing his or her business and I believe we are better equipped than anyone to make a massive difference to them.

What's strange is that it all began with a big mistake …

CHAPTER 14
IT COULDN'T BE DONE

So that's my story – so far! – and those are my rules. (I've listed them together on pages 244–45 for easy reference.)

How much that bump on the ceiling during the '66 World Cup Final is to blame for everything, I guess we'll never know. I'm sure the psychologists will say that it's a legacy of my coma and/or coming to terms with my own mortality at such an early age that contributes to my drive and ambition, but I don't think so. There are plenty of people who've achieved more success in business than I have without such trauma. It's not a requirement!

There really is nothing special about me. Anyone can do what I've done. Sure, I have plenty of energy and drive, but so can you!

Yes, I've become pretty good at implementing what I have learnt into my business – and you can, too!

When I started out on my own, and formed N5, I was singularly ill equipped to succeed as an entrepreneur. I'd had a 'corporate' life. I wasn't streetwise. There was so much I didn't know.

Fortunately, looking back, I think that the single most important contributor to my success was my ability to recognise my own incompetence. Seriously. I was sufficiently self-aware to realise that I had a heck of lot to learn – and I set out to learn it.

I do 'learn' a lot, every day, even now. In my experience, most business owners don't make any kind of commitment to learning new things. The notion of actually reading a business book is completely alien to many. (Congratulations, by the way, because reading this one business book puts you into the 'way above average' set!)

Yet most business owners also don't achieve the level of success that they aspired to when they set out.

No learning. Less success.

Lots of learning. Lots of success.

Coincidence? I don't think so.

I wish I'd had **Botty's Rules** on day one. I'm not suggesting that they are a completely comprehensive set of guidelines for someone in business but what I do know is that pretty much every super-successful business owner I've ever met follows 'em, and they would have been darned useful to me in those early years.

Adopting and following **Botty's Rules** has certainly been a critical factor in my business – especially over the last couple of years when we have continued to flourish and grow despite the economic turmoil that has caused so many problems for other business owners.

If your ambition is to have a 'lifestyle' business – one that pays you 40 or 50 grand a year, then you can probably afford to ignore many of the rules. But if your ambition is more than that, if you want to build something that is super-successful, long-lasting and that can make you rich, then **Botty's Rules** are both a blue-print and a scorecard for you.

But … you've got to take action! Start by using the checklist on pages 244–45 to identify which **Botty Rules** you need to focus on first. Just pick three or four to begin with (bite-sized goals, remember) and make some progress with them.

That will start to build momentum, and momentum is incredibly powerful in business.

Of course, the best and most impactful way for you to make progress towards full compliance with **Botty's Rules** – and to rapidly accelerate the growth of your business – is to join my 'gang'. You're welcome to take a free trial of my Entrepreneurs' Circle any time. It's for UK business owners who want to be super-successful.

If you're interested, go to **www.nigelbotterill.com/ bookoffer**.

One final story before I finish.

Remember Frances White from Chapter 1? She was the coach that Barclays employed who helped me realise that I needed to become an entrepreneur. Well, one day, Frances gave me a copy of a poem. I framed it, and it's held pride of place above my desk ever since.

It was written by a guy called Edgar Guest who was born, in 1881, only four miles from where I now live.

Every day the poem inspires me. It's been with me throughout my entire entrepreneurial journey. It's been with me throughout my discovery and formulation of **Botty's Rules** – and all the ups and downs of my story.

It captures the attitude and approach that I strive each day to manifest. It's helped me stay strong when things haven't gone well – and it's fuelled my fire when we've been on a roll.

I hope it inspires and helps you, too. It seemed a fitting way to end this book.

Good luck on your journey – Britain needs us entrepreneurs more than ever right now – and whenever anyone tells you it can't be done, just smile and read this poem …

It Couldn't Be Done

Somebody said that it couldn't be done,
But he with a chuckle replied
That 'maybe it couldn't', but he would be one
Who wouldn't say so till he'd tried.
So, he buckled right in with the trace of a grin
On his face, if he worried he hid it.
He started to sing as he tackled the thing
That couldn't be done, as he did it.

Somebody scoffed: 'Oh, you'll never do that;
At least no one ever has done it';
But he took off his coat and he took off his hat,
And the first thing we knew he'd begun it.
With a lift of his chin and a bit of a grin,
Without any doubting or quiddit,
He started to sing as he tackled the thing
That couldn't be done, and he did it.

There are thousands to tell you it cannot be done,
There are thousands to prophesy failure;
There are thousands to point out to you, one by one,
The dangers that wait to assail you.
But just buckle in with a bit of a grin,
Just take off your coat and go to it;
Just start to sing as you tackle the thing
That 'cannot be done', and you'll do it.

EDGAR ALBERT GUEST, 1881–1959

BOTTY'S RULES CHECKLIST

	Doing okay	Needs work
1. Take 100% responsibility (page 28)	☐	☐
2. Who you hang around with matters. A lot (page 33)	☐	☐
3. Residual income is a beautiful thing (page 40)	☐	☐
4. Attitude is everything (page 48)	☐	☐
5. Deadlines get stuff done (page 55)	☐	☐
6. Good is good enough (page 57)	☐	☐
7. Become a 'marketer' *not* a doer (page 65)	☐	☐
8. To get high income, just get more done (page 70)	☐	☐
9. Follow up, follow up, follow up (page 75)	☐	☐
10. Exploit the web fully – 'cos most people aren't! (page 82)	☐	☐
11. Most people in your industry or sector are wrong … about everything (page 92)	☐	☐
12. Getting and keeping customers – your first job every day (page 102)	☐	☐
13. 'I think big. Most people think small. This gives me a distinct advantage' (page 114)	☐	☐

BOTTY'S RULES CHECKLIST

	Doing okay	*Needs work*
14. There is no status quo (page 119)	☐	☐
15. Make money or make excuses – but you can't do both (page 131)	☐	☐
16. S**t happens – and it always will (page 142)	☐	☐
17. Give customers the chance to buy a premium-priced product (page 148)	☐	☐
18. Pay-per-Click – one of the most powerful business tools ever (page 158)	☐	☐
19. No one cares as much as you (page 162)	☐	☐
20. Bite-sized goals are good (page 167)	☐	☐
21. You've got to stop the sabotage (page 182)	☐	☐
22. The power of testimonials (page 193)	☐	☐
23. Working ON your business, not in it! (page 198)	☐	☐
24. Social media is changing everything (page 202)	☐	☐
25. Good offers make you money (page 205)	☐	☐
26. Only lazy, incompetent business owners don't know how well each bit of their marketing works (page 212)	☐	☐
27. Your most valuable asset – bar none – is your database (page 217)	☐	☐
28. Speed matters (page 232)	☐	☐
29. The single biggest thing you can do (page 235)	☐	☐

AN OFFER FROM NIGEL BOTTERILL

for readers of *Botty's Rules*

Dear reader,

First of all, thank you for reading my book. I never set out to be a published author, in fact, I had to be encouraged, cajoled and pushed into putting pen to paper and sharing my story. Now you've finished it (and I hope that you enjoyed it), we come to something of a fork in the road.

This can be the end, or a beginning.

If you've found my book interesting and useful, then I've got good news for you. There's plenty more where this came from.

You see, I write thousands of words each and every month, sent out in a regular newsletter and by email to thousands of entrepreneurs and business owners right across the UK. I'm on stage most months, presenting the latest findings from my own business to hundreds of other business owners. I run webinars and spend hours on the phone each week working with entrepreneurs on THEIR businesses.

All this is available to members of my private 'Entrepreneurs' Circle', an exclusive club for some of the UK's smartest small business owners (maybe just like you?).

If you've found this book to be interesting and engaging, then I **know** you'll take a whole lot more value from being a member of my Entrepreneurs' Circle – which is why I'm offering you this free gift ...

**Take the Entrepreneurs' Circle for a two-month 'test drive'.
Sample everything from the newsletter to a live event, completely FREE, and with no obligation whatsoever.**

After two whole months you can decide for yourself whether you want your membership to continue.

Watch the video that I've recorded especially for you at www.nigelbotterill.com/bookoffer

I sincerely hope that you make the right choice at this fork in the road. If you've enjoyed my story, and found the lessons in this book to be valuable, I hope that you'll join me, and we'll meet or speak together soon.

For full details and to accept my gift of a free-two-month test drive of my Entrepreneurs' Circle, visit:

www.nigelbotterill.com/bookoffer

Whatever you decide, I wish you well on your business journey.

Offer is subject to change without notice.
Small shipping/handling charge applies.